Praise for *Redeeming Productivity*

This is what a time management book should be: theological, theoretical, *and* tactical. *Redeeming Productivity* is a great, gospel-centric book!

JORDAN RAYNOR, national bestselling author of *Redeeming Your Time: 7 Biblical Principles for Being Purposeful, Present, and Wildly Productive*

Before I entered pastoral ministry, I spent several years working in the business world. In keeping step with other successful businessmen in my office, I read numerous books on how to increase sales, manage my time, stay motivated, and make lots of money. However, none of these practices truly helped me or gave glory to God. In many ways, if felt like I was running on a hamster wheel, chasing productivity but not really knowing why. As I grew in my knowledge and love of the Lord, my focus began to change. Having had this previous experience, I was overjoyed and thankful to read Reagan Rose's book *Redeeming Productivity*. He gives voice to the issue of being productive, not simply for one's own good, but for God's ultimate glory. Not only does Reagan give a bevy of helpful tools for personal efficiency, but he grounds the whole book in the Word of God. This is an invaluable resource that I wish I had two decades ago. However, I'm glad it's here now!

NATE PICKOWICZ, Teaching Pastor, Harvest Bible Church, Gilmanton Iron Works, NH; author, *How to Eat Your Bible*

Followers of Christ have bought into a worldly view of productivity. We think life is about us and getting more stuff done. In his book *Redeeming Productivity*, Reagan Rose helps us better understand how to be productive for God's glory and the good of others. *Redeeming Productivity* is a perfect combination of right thinking and practical application. I wish I had this book fifteen years ago!

SCOTT KEDERSHA, marriage pastor at Harris Creek Baptist Church and author of *Ready or Knot: 12 Conversations Every Couple Needs to Have before Marriage*

For the past couple of years, I've been learning everything I can from Reagan Rose. I'm not exaggerating when I say that his wisdom has changed my life. I'm excited to see him share his knowledge in this excellent book. Just as I expected, it's clear, biblical, and practical. Read this book. Mark it up. Most of all, apply its lessons. I'm confident that you will benefit from Reagan's wisdom too.

DARRYL DASH, pastor of Liberty Grace Church, Toronto; author of
8 Habits for Growth

Our lives belong to Christ, not ourselves. That is the first principle of productivity for Christians—and Reagan Rose shows us how it changes everything. This much-needed book is filled with outstanding tips and techniques. But most importantly, it grounds everything in a sound theology of why we need to be productive at all.

MATT PERMAN, author, *What's Best Next: How the Gospel Transforms the Way You Get Things Done* and *How to Get Unstuck*

Fruitful labor is a gift from the Lord as He graciously works in and through His people for His good pleasure. Productivity is not so much a science to be studied but a prayerful discipline to cultivate, entrusting our service to the faithful Lord of the harvest who is always working in our lives, in our families, in our churches, and in our communities. In this insightful book, Reagan Rose distills biblical wisdom as we pursue productivity not for our glory, but for God alone.

CHRIS LARSON, President & CEO, Ligonier Ministries

Getting More Done for the Glory of God

REDEEMING PRODUCTIVITY

REAGAN ROSE

MOODY PUBLISHERS
CHICAGO

Some content in chapters 1 and 2 was adapted from material previously published by the author at redeemingproductivity.com.

Edited by Charles Snyder
Interior design: Puckett Smartt
Cover design: Erik M. Peterson
Cover illustration of leaves copyright © 2020 by Valeriia Soloveva / Shutterstock (1927551848).
Cover illustration of hour glass copyright © 2020 by Fernandi Putra / Shutterstock (1698162133).
All rights reserved for both of the illustrations above.
Author photo credit: Ema Capoccia

Library of Congress Cataloging-in-Publication Data

Names: Rose, Reagan, author.
Title: Redeeming productivity : getting more done for the glory of God /
   Reagan Rose.
Description: Chicago, IL : Moody Publishers, [2022] | Includes
   bibliographical references. | Summary: "The world says be productive so
   that you can get all you can out of this life. The Bible says be
   productive so you can gain more of the next life. Rose explores how only
   through our relationship to Christ-the True Vine-are we empowered to
   produce good fruit"-- Provided by publisher.
Identifiers: LCCN 2022021700 (print) | LCCN 2022021701 (ebook) | ISBN
   9780802428943 (paperback) | ISBN 9780802474636 (ebook)
Subjects: LCSH: Work--Religious aspects--Christianity. | Production
   (Economic theory) | BISAC: RELIGION / Christian Living / Professional
   Growth | RELIGION / Christian Living / Leadership & Mentoring
Classification: LCC BT738.5 .R573 2022 (print) | LCC BT738.5 (ebook) |
   DDC 248.8/8--dc23/eng/20220606
LC record available at https://lccn.loc.gov/2022021700
LC ebook record available at https://lccn.loc.gov/2022021701

Originally delivered by fleets of horse-drawn wagons, the affordable paperbacks from D. L. Moody's publishing house resourced the church and served everyday people. Now, after more than 125 years of publishing and ministry, Moody Publishers' mission remains the same—even if our delivery systems have changed a bit. For more information on other books (and resources) created from a biblical perspective, go to www.moodypublishers.com or write to:

Moody Publishers
820 N. LaSalle Boulevard
Chicago, IL 60610

1 3 5 7 9 10 8 6 4 2

Printed in the United States of America

This book is dedicated to my mother, Dianne Rose,
a wise counselor and a faithful example.

CONTENTS

FOREWORD

Productivity is a wonderful servant, but a terrible master. Productivity can serve us so well or treat us so poorly. No wonder, then, that so many of us have a love-hate relationship with it. No wonder, then, that so many of us have learned to be suspicious of books and methods that promise to increase and enhance our productivity. For we have so often tried them and found them wanting.

I find myself increasingly grateful for a new generation of productivity writers—people like Reagan Rose—who are attempting to redeem productivity from its many pretenders. Reagan has come to see that most modern-day methodologies are intrinsically selfish, attempts to serve oneself without serving others. But by looking through a biblical lens, he understands that productivity is at its best when it is turned outward, when it is about faithfully stewarding the life God has assigned to each of us.

So while Reagan does teach productivity, and while he gets as granular as specific methodologies, he does so for the very clear purpose of helping us know how we can best live our lives for the great and wonderful purpose of bringing glory to God. This is the life of true meaning, of true significance, and of true satisfaction.

I would invite you to read *Redeeming Productivity* and, through it, to learn not only why you should live for the purpose of glorifying God, but also to learn how you can do so deliberately, confidently, and creatively.

TIM CHALLIES
www.challies.com
www.twitter.com/challies
www.facebook.com/challies

INTRODUCTION

——— ‐ ‐ ———

Productivity has been hijacked, and it's time we take it back.

Browse the self-help section at any bookstore and you're likely to find some common themes on the dust jackets. The message is always some variation of how you can get richer, happier, or become more successful if you just learn how to get more done.

The problem with these books is they work. If you learn to manage your calendar better, block out your tasks, and make the most of your peak hours of energy, yes, you will get more done. I say this is a problem because the techniques taught in these books rarely come alone. Often hiding behind practical tips on time management, decision-making, or goal setting is a whole spectrum of worldly philosophies. Productivity books don't just tell us how to work, they tell us *why* we work. They assume definitions for success, meaning, and effectiveness that run contrary to the Bible. And even Christians, if we aren't careful, can start to believe those things too.

We all want to get more done. But for Christians, *why* we get more done is just as important as how. So, the aim of this book is to address both the why and the how of productivity so you can get more done for the glory of God.

In the pages ahead I lay a foundation for thinking biblically about work and efficiency. This foundation consists of what I call the five pillars of Christian productivity. They address the origin, purpose, content, power, and motivation for being productive. Each pillar has to do with a specific aspect of our relationship with God and how that informs the way we think about productivity. Only when we have our theological foundation right can we start to build productive practices that truly honor God.

But this book is not just theoretical. It also looks at the *how* of personal productivity. After each pillar, we will explore a practice that pairs with that pillar's theme. You may have heard of some of these practices before, but here they have been adapted to better fit within a Christian worldview. Other practices will likely be completely new to you. But all of them have been chosen deliberately because I believe them to be the five most effective productivity habits.

My desire is that this book would help Christians reclaim a more thoughtful theology and practice of productivity, one that is rooted in the Scriptures and doggedly committed to honoring God. You can learn to be more productive without sacrificing your biblical convictions. May this book give you a clearer vision of our great God and energize you to press on productively for His sake. Because the work we do in this life truly matters. And if we do our work well, His way, resting fully in the gospel of Jesus Christ, that work will redound to His glory and our good throughout all eternity.

1

THE ORIGIN OF PRODUCTIVITY

You Belong to God

⸻ – – ⸻

Over the past ten years, I've gone deep down the self-help rabbit hole. I've read all the most influential books on personal productivity, studied the various theories of time management, and experimented with just about every productivity trend and tool you can think of. And since 2016, I've been writing and teaching about personal productivity from a Christian worldview. But I haven't always been interested in this topic. In fact, for a long time I thought the subject was decidedly *unchristian*. And when I did finally take an interest in my own productivity, it was for all the wrong reasons. I now see that the reason I didn't think productivity mattered and the reason I first took an interest in it were both rooted in the same lie: "it's my life."

"It's my life" is a radical and often rebellious mode of thinking. It's the attitude behind our insistence that we don't owe anything to anyone and that no one can tell us what to do. My life is my possession to do with as I choose. And "it's my life" is the fundamental assumption behind the spirit of our age. It's in the movies we watch, the books we read, and in the background of every secular work on productivity. We are constantly bombarded with the lie, "It's my life, so I can use it however I want." This self-centered philosophy leads to all manner of woes, but it also happens to be the root of two opposite conclusions we might draw about the place personal productivity should hold in our lives. And I should know because I've fallen for both.

TWO WAYS WE GET IT WRONG

The first way "it's my life" thinking can lead us astray is by causing us to believe productivity is entirely unimportant. If you had met me at the beginning of my college career, you would certainly not have said, "Now there's a guy interested in personal productivity!" Quite the opposite, in fact—I was overweight, addicted to video games, and without purpose or ambition in the world. I had no idea who I was, why I was here, or where I was going. And I didn't care.

What made my state even more pathetic was that I was arrogant about it. Ambition and productivity were for people in suits with fake smiles and the word "entrepreneur" on their business cards. Why would I want to be like *those* people? If they wanted to pursue their little careers to make them happy, fine. But what was that to me? Leave me alone and let me do what makes *me* happy. And what made me happy was *Halo 3* and Flaming Hot Cheetos. To me, my logic seemed airtight: we are all just trying to do what makes us happy. So, what difference does it make if someone searches for happiness through business, gaming, or even trapeze artistry? It's my life.

In part, I was right. If those productivity-minded sales bros who I had such contempt for were only pursuing productivity for worldly success, then we weren't all that different. We were both believing the "it's my life" lie and just drawing different conclusions from it. I had concluded that since it's my life, productivity was a matter of preference. Maybe this is how you think about productivity too—a fine thing to pursue if you care to, but not something you need to worry about.

The second way "it's my life" thinking expresses itself regarding personal productivity is in prioritizing productivity for the wrong reasons. Many people, some Christians included, see productivity merely as a vehicle for helping them create the life that will make them most happy. And this vision of productivity is exactly what most self-improvement resources propagate. I'm embarrassed to say it, but this motivation is why I first became interested in productivity. From the outside it appeared I had turned a leaf, but really, I was the same person. Now, instead of being lazy because I believed "it's my life," I wanted to get more done because "it's my life." It was still all about me.

Halfway through my undergraduate degree program, I transferred schools and determined to reinvent myself. I decided I was going to get As, start eating healthy, get in shape, and really become someone. Driven by this newfound determination, I got deep into the productivity genre. I shoveled every podcast, book, and blog on productivity into my brain. I couldn't get enough of the stuff. And guess what—the things I learned really did work!

I lost weight, got a girlfriend, became more confident, and even got better grades—just like the gurus promised. But all the while I was unknowingly drinking theological poison. Reading all that stuff on productivity hadn't just been teaching me how to get more done. Behind every tip for managing my time, setting effective goals, or creating lasting habits was that same underlying assumption: "it's my life." The motivation for working harder and getting more done was always so *I* could become happier, *I* could be more successful, or *I* could get richer. The focus was always *me*. *This is the origin of all unchristian productivity. It is a selfish desire for self-improvement for self's sake.*

First, we need to redeem the origin of productivity. I don't mean the history of the personal productivity movement, though we will look at that more in chapter 5. I mean the origin of a person's desire to get more done. Maybe, like me, you have read all the productivity classics, can't stand wasting time, and are borderline obsessed with performing tasks in the most efficient way possible. Or maybe you are deeply suspicious of personal productivity. You consider it the domain of wannabe millionaires or neurotic type A people, not something Christians should give heed to. I want to show you that Christians *should* care about personal productivity and *why* we should care.

The first pillar of productivity that must be redeemed is the origin of our productivity. The world says you belong to yourself. But the Bible says your life is a stewardship from God, a gift that must be used in service to God for His glory. Acknowledging this fundamental difference will help us pursue productivity in a way that honors God by putting Him first, not ourselves.

DEFINING PRODUCTIVITY

Before we get too far along, let me give a definition for what I mean when I say "productivity." Throughout this book, unless otherwise noted, the word "productivity" refers to *personal* productivity. Which is to say, this is not a book about the output of farms, factories, companies, or machines. We're talking about people.

When it comes to books, the genre we call "productivity" encompasses a variety of subjects. Type "productivity" into Amazon and you'll find works on time management, to-do lists, goal setting, prioritization, and much more. But at a basic level, when modern people talk about personal productivity, they are usually talking about how efficiently and consistently an individual can complete important tasks. This is how I plan to use the word in this book. Productivity is about efficiently accomplishing the right things. My contention is that what those things are, why you want to accomplish them, and what it means to do so efficiently should be different for Christians, considering what the Scriptures teach about our relationship to God.

Tips, Tricks & Philosophy

Several years ago, I was on vacation with my wife, Kim, in Lake Arrowhead, California. I had just finished seminary and my thoughts were on the future. Where was I going? What did I want to do? How could I best serve God with my gifts? I was praying and searching the Scriptures, but I was also looking for advice in books on goal setting, planning, and personal productivity.

One afternoon, after taking a walk by the lake, we came back to our cabin to rest for a little while before dinner. I stretched out on the couch, the scent of pine still fresh in my nostrils and the relaxing songs of birds drifting through the cracked windows. I took a deep breath and hit play on a new audiobook I'd downloaded just before the trip.

I hadn't been listening for long before the author said something that caught my attention. He was quoting his mentor, saying, "He taught me that life is simply a collection of experiences; our goal should be to increase the frequency and the intensity of the good experiences."[1] I nodded approvingly and whispered aloud, "Ooh, that's good." I started looking around the room for my pen and notebook so I could write it down. Then I caught myself.

The problem?

Describing the goal of life as increasing the frequency and intensity of good experiences is almost the dictionary definition of hedonism. This is how Webster defines hedonism: "the doctrine that pleasure or happiness is the sole or chief good in life."[2] There I was, a Bible-believing, fancy-shmancy seminary graduate, feeling ready to take on the world for Christ, and I was merrily nodding along to the tenets of pagan philosophy wrapped in a modern productivity book. The worst part of it all is I had been writing my blog on personal productivity from a Christian perspective for three years at this point. The whole purpose of that blog was to expose and correct this kind of unbiblical thinking about productivity! And yet I still fell prey to the "it's my life" philosophy of productivity.

I wish I could say this was the only time I had that experience while reading a book on productivity, but it wasn't. Between the practical tips and tricks, authors of books like these can't help but insert their philosophy of life. You simply cannot speak about productivity very long before talking about why we care about it. And the origin of a Christian's interest in productivity ought to be radically different from that of a person who does not know Christ. No matter how you slice it, we want to be productive either to serve ourselves or to serve God. And as much as I love and continue to benefit from books, podcasts, and blogs on productivity produced by secular authors, I've learned I can't let my guard down. Every philosophy of productivity contains a theology.

ME-CENTERED MOTIVATION

While every author may not state it as plainly as the one I just quoted, the most common unbiblical idea you'll find in nearly every work on productivity is a me-centered motivation. We call it *self*-improvement for a reason. The promise is that you can have more success, more money, more respect, more peace, and more happiness if you can learn to get more done. It's an appealing proposition. Just imagine how amazing your life would be if you got everything under control!

Don't get me wrong. It's not that there's something wrong with wanting to improve yourself—the book in your hands is unabashedly concerned with helping you improve. But whether you're seeking to advance your career, get in better shape, or simply learn to manage your time more effectively, the goodness of those pursuits hinges on their *why*. Do I care about productivity because I want to make the most of my life for Christ? Or do I care about it because I want a killer beach bod and a Lambo? We must be discerning when it comes to our own hearts. And that begins by rooting our basic beliefs about productivity not just in who we are, but in *whose* we are. If you are a Christian, you belong to Christ. Your life is not your own.

The world says you belong to yourself, but the Bible says you belong to God. This fundamental truth is the first pillar of Christian productivity. But far from stopping us from caring about productivity, I believe it is the strongest motive for pursuing it.

NOT YOUR LIFE, BUT HIS

We will reference John 15 frequently throughout this book. This passage comes as part of Jesus' Farewell Discourse the night before His crucifixion, and He delivered these remarks to the eleven remaining disciples immediately after the last supper. In this chapter, Jesus speaks of Himself as "the true vine" and His followers as "the branches." This is one of the most important passages in the New Testament about the believer's union with Christ. This union, which is ours by faith, is the basis of our right standing before God the Father and our shared inheritance of every spiritual blessing and promise of God. But our union with Christ is also the basis for all God-honoring productivity.

There are several interesting observations about productivity and the Christian that we can make in this chapter. John 15:5 says, "I am the vine; you are the branches. Whoever abides in me and I in him, he it is that bears much fruit, for apart from me you can do nothing." Those who are in Christ "bear much fruit." Or, we could say, Christians are productive. We'll look much more at the nature of this fruit and what the relationship between vine and branches says about Christian productivity in later chapters. But for now, I want to note what this passage indicates about the origin of our productivity. Christian productivity is not primarily about who we are, but whose we are. Christian productivity begins by acknowledging that we belong to Christ.

It's *not* my life. It's His.

If you believe in Jesus Christ, you belong to God. That's why we call Him Lord. It's an act of submission to His claim on every aspect of our lives, including our work, our ambitions, how we manage our time, and everything in between. The apostle Paul couldn't have put it more plainly: "*You are not your own,* for you were bought with a price. So glorify God in your body" (1 Cor. 6:19b–20). It's not your life because you were bought and paid for. To redeem productivity, therefore, we must begin by considering our own redemption.

To redeem literally means to buy back, pay a ransom for, or reclaim as one's own. You see the concept of redemption in the Old Testament "right of redemption." According to Mosaic law, a person had the right, under certain conditions, to purchase back a piece of family land that had previously been sold (see Lev. 25:25–29 and Jer. 32:7–8). The plotline of the book of Ruth centers on this kind of redemption. The story culminates with Boaz marrying Ruth and purchasing back the land that would have belonged to her deceased husband, because another relative refused to redeem it for her (Ruth 4:6). Boaz is said to be acting on Ruth's behalf as a "kinsman-redeemer"—someone with the right and responsibility to rescue a relative from poverty or trouble (Ruth 3:9; 4:9, 10; see also Lev. 25:47–55). But the biblical concept of redemption goes beyond real estate.

In the ancient world, one could buy back prisoners of war. If you paid the price, you had the right to redeem your people from an enemy nation. This was true of slaves as well. When the New Testament speaks of believers being redeemed by Jesus Christ, it's using this concept in a spiritual sense. When God redeems a sinner, He is buying us back from the slave market of sin. Your price has been paid. So, if your price has been paid, does that mean you are free? Yes, in a sense. Redeemed people are set free from sin, but now they belong to a new master. Romans 6:22 says, "You have been set free from sin and have become slaves of God." You were bought by God. Now He is your Lord and Master. You belong to Him, and so does the work of your hands. Now, instead of offering our productive efforts to be used for unrighteous and self-gratifying work, we offer them to our new Master for His work. "Do not present your members to sin as instruments for unrighteousness, but present yourselves to God as those who have been brought from death to life, and your members to God as instruments for righteousness" (Rom. 6:13). But to fully appreciate how amazing this transformation is, we must recall that redemption always requires payment. And the price of our spiritual redemption was steep.

YOU WEREN'T CHEAP

Knowing the high price God paid for our redemption should engender a sense of obligation in us. To be clear, God does not expect us to repay grace (nor could we ever hope to). Salvation is a gift; we contribute nothing to it. But notice that Paul links our purchase price to a command: "For you were bought with a price. So glorify God in your body" (1 Cor. 6:20). The price of our redemption should logically lead to us wanting to glorify God. Often, we don't feel the weight of that obligation because we don't dwell on just how expensive the price of redemption was. The price for our redemption was the blood of Jesus Christ.

In Ephesians, the apostle Paul writes, "In him we have redemption through his blood" (Eph. 1:7). Paul similarly describes the church as being "purchased with his own blood" (Acts 20:28 KJV). We weren't cheap. God poured out His wrath on His only begotten Son, sending Him to the cross to suffer and die on our behalf, then raising Him again from the dead so that the Father might buy us back for Himself. You were bought and paid for with the most precious currency in the universe—the blood of the Son of God. This is cause for thankfulness and rejoicing, for it means that our sins are forgiven, we have a right standing before God, and we have the sure hope of heaven (Col. 1:14; Rom. 3:24; Heb. 9:15). Reflecting on the price of your redemption should cause you to weep with joy. But it should also cause you to treat your life not as your own but as a precious stewardship from God. As Charles Spurgeon put it, "Your whole manhood belongs to God if you are a Christian. Every faculty, every natural power, every talent, every possibility of your being, every capacity of your spirit—all were bought."[3]

PRODUCTIVITY IS LIFE STEWARDSHIP

When Christians hear the word stewardship, we often think of money. We think of giving to the church, investing wisely, and not wasting our money. But financial stewardship, though important, is only one aspect of a Christian's responsibility to God. If we belong to God, our whole lives are a stewardship, not just our wallets.

Jesus talks about stewardship in the parable of the talents. Speaking of the kingdom of heaven, He says, "For it will be like a man going on a journey, who called his servants and entrusted to them his property. To one he gave five talents, to another two, to another one, to each according to his ability. Then he went away" (Matt. 25:14–15). We call those men the master had look after his affairs stewards. A steward is simply someone charged with looking after something on behalf of someone else. In the same way, God has charged us to look after our lives which He has purchased by the blood of Jesus Christ.

Understood this way, personal productivity ceases to be a way to get the most out of life for my sake. Instead, it becomes the set of tools I use to skillfully execute the stewardship I've been given. How do I best invest my years, months, hours, and moments to make the greatest return for my Master? How do I best care for my health, mind, and opportunities such that they are employed as productively as possible in God's service?

Life stewardship will look different for every individual, and each of us will be given different things to steward, but the core principles stay the same. In the parable of the talents, the master entrusts money to the three servants "each according to his ability," then he leaves (v. 15). Here is the first principle: we aren't all given the same amount to steward. Some will have greater talents, some more money, some greater health, some more energy. Viewed this way, stewardship also eliminates jealousy.

I once heard the pastor of a small congregation humbly thank God that He had not given him more congregants than he could faithfully look after. This man understood he would give an account for the souls that God had entrusted to him. So instead of looking jealously at the megachurch down the road and grumbling that he didn't have their pastor's magnetic personality, as gifted a worship team, or as nice of a facility, he just decided to be faithful with what he had. The same should be true of us with our productivity. It's not about competing to be the best or most productive. It's about making the most of what the Lord has given us.

In the story of the talents, the first two servants invest their master's money and make a handy return for him: "He who had received the five talents went at once and traded with them, and he made five talents more. So also he who had the two talents made two talents more" (vv. 16–17). But the final steward did nothing with what he'd been given. "But he who had received the one talent went and dug in the ground and hid his master's money" (v. 18). When the master returns, he rewards the first two and punishes the last. Why? This is the second principle of stewardship: stewards have a responsibility to make a good return on whatever has been entrusted to them, whether big or small.

Some people have all the talent, money, and opportunity in the world. They are privileged beyond imagination. We look at their energy, their zeal, and all that they can achieve and say, "Wow, I could never be that productive." But the truth is you aren't in a race against them. God is only concerned with how you stewarded what was entrusted to you. All you need to worry about is being faithful. Productivity for you might not look like waking up early, crushing it at the gym, and serving in six different ministries, all while holding down two jobs and raising a family. For a steward, productivity just means being faithful with what you've been given.

So, should Christians care about productivity? Absolutely! But the reason we care about it should be unique. I love the way R. C. Sproul put it: "Our calling as Christians is the highest calling there is, and the idea of being productive is not the invention of capitalism; it is the mandate of Christ."[4] The first pillar of a redeemed productivity, therefore, is its origin. The world says "it's your life," but God says "you belong to Me."

In the next chapter we will look at a daily practice that is the cornerstone of any productive life. We'll see how to put life stewardship into action by giving God the firstfruits of our day.

CRAFT YOUR MORNING ROUTINE

——— – – ———

It's Monday morning.

Your alarm sounds. You wake up and roll out of bed. You didn't hit snooze because you've had enough sleep. You feel well rested. It's still early. The house is quiet. No one else is awake yet.

After splashing some water on your face, you make a cup of coffee and settle into your favorite chair. On the side table sits your Bible, already opened to the next passage in your reading plan. You read it. Then you spend some time in prayer, worshiping God, confessing sin, thanking Him, and praying for the day ahead.

Next, you stand up to do a few jumping jacks, just to get the blood flowing. The caffeine is starting to hit. You're really feeling awake now. You sit back down and read a few pages in one of your other books and write in your journal.

Now, you look at your calendar to see what's on the agenda for the day. You lay out your plan of attack, the tasks you'll tackle, and you anticipate where you're most likely to be distracted. You're feeling ready. You're actually looking forward to the day ahead. You feel prepared to live this day well for the glory of God.

And you did all of this before anyone else woke up.

Imagine if that was your morning routine. Imagine how energized you'd feel, how relaxed, and how ready you'd be to tackle the day's tasks. Now imagine what your life would look like if you did that consistently for a month, a year, five years. What would your spiritual life look like? Your career? Your home? What kind of person would you become if you had a strategic plan for starting your day?

I believe a morning routine is a keystone habit of any productive life. "Keystone habit" is the term Charles Duhigg uses to describe those "small changes or habits that people introduce into their routines that unintentionally carry over into other aspects of their lives."[1] If you get your morning routine right, you'll find many other good habits beginning to line up behind it. In this chapter, I'll show you how almost anyone can implement a better morning routine, teach you how to make it Christ-centered, and give you a step-by-step plan for getting started first thing tomorrow.

MORNING ROUTINES CHANGED MY LIFE

Since I write and talk about productivity for a living, I often get asked some version of the question, "What's your number one productivity tip?" And while there are dozens of practices I could recommend that can help someone become a better steward of their time, the answer I give is the always the same: start with your mornings.

The reason I'm so passionate about morning routines is because over the past ten years, the simple routine I'll show you in this chapter has completely transformed my life. The consistent act of getting up a little earlier and going through a fixed schedule of activities before my day begins has allowed me to:

- Develop a close and consistent walk with the Lord
- Read 50+ books per year
- Enjoy a more focused and deliberate working life
- Create a successful blog and podcast in my spare time

I'm not saying that stuff to brag. My point is that I'm not special. I'm not even an especially disciplined person by nature. I simply carved out some extra time in the mornings and was deliberate with how I spent it. Anyone who does that and sticks with it for a long period of time will experience amazing results.

Someone once said the first hour of the morning is the rudder of the day. Like the rudder on a ship, your mornings are a relatively small part of your day, but they set the direction. A well-crafted, Christ-first morning routine is the best way I've found to begin a productive day.

I can hear your eyes rolling now. You're thinking, "Mornings are hard enough already, Reagan! You want me to wake up even *earlier*?" Believe me, I get it. I wasn't always a morning person myself. And I doubt I would have ever chosen the morning life. You could say the morning life chose me.

Before I married Kim, I was a card-carrying member of the night owl society. I loved staying up late. If you knew me back then, I would have told you I did my best work late at night. I cherished the quiet, focused late-night hours, often staying up well past midnight. Of course, I usually ended up paying for those late nights the following day. But I loved the creativity and the lack of pressure that came from working on projects while everyone else was asleep.

When we got married, Kim and I made the decision to always go to bed at the same time. I could probably write a whole book on the many benefits that single decision has had for our marriage, but one unexpected blessing was that it turned me into a morning person. You see, my wife needs a lot more sleep than I do, about nine hours. But I've found that I function best on about seven hours of sleep. So, when we started going to bed at 9:30 each night, I found myself—quite unintentionally—waking up at 4:30 a.m. At first, I tried to fight it. I thought it was insomnia. I'd lie in bed telling myself, "You can't get up yet, 4:30 is way too early!" Eventually, however, I did the math. 9:30 p.m. to 4:30 a.m. I was getting my seven hours. I was getting enough sleep. So I started getting out of bed at four-have-I-lost-my-mind-thirty in the morning every day. And to be honest, waking up early wasn't that helpful at first. I still didn't know what to do with that extra time.

Suddenly I had a whole heap of undistracted time at my disposal. Initially I thought I just needed to find a way to occupy myself until the real day started. I'd flip on the TV or get on social media until the sun rose. But one day it hit me that I'd been given an amazing gift: focused time. Everyone always says they wish they had more time to get things done, and I actually had my hands on the precious stuff and was just squandering it. So I started testing out a variety of different morning routines to make the most of this treasure.

I'll show you in a moment what I've found to be the most fruitful activities to fill your mornings with. And no, you do not need to wake up at 4:30 a.m. to implement or benefit from a routine like this. I will recommend, however, that you start with waking thirty minutes earlier than normal. If you're like many others I've taught this morning routine to, once you start experiencing the benefits of it, you'll find yourself wanting to wake up even earlier. But before I introduce the elements of this particular morning routine, I want to show you why I think mornings are usually the most preferrable time for productive activities.

THE FIRSTFRUITS OF THE DAY

If you type in "morning routine" on YouTube, you'll be treated with a generous assortment of cringe-inducing videos that promise to help you become a millionaire by copying what Elon Musk or Jeff Bezos supposedly do upon waking. It is true that if you study the life of nearly any successful person, you'll usually find a rigorous morning routine. However, while temporal success is not necessarily a bad thing, both the content of and the reason for a Christian's morning routine should come from his or her identity in Christ. As we saw in the previous chapter, a Christian's desire to be productive originates in the acknowledgment that he or she belongs to God. As a blood-bought child of God, your life is a living sacrifice (Rom. 12:1). And the first thing you do when you roll out of bed in the morning is your first act of worship for the day.

The Bible talks about this principle as "firstfruits." The idea is that God expected His people to offer Him the first and best of their productivity. "The best of the firstfruits of your ground you shall bring to the house of the LORD your God" (Ex. 34:26). Whether you were growing grain (Lev. 2:14) or raising livestock (Deut. 12:6), whether you were rich or poor (Num. 12:20), God's people were to give Him the firstfruits of their labor. "Honor the LORD with your wealth and with the firstfruits of all your produce" (Prov. 3:9).

By giving God the first and best of what you had produced, you were acknowledging that it all belongs to Him anyway. And while we no longer practice the sacrificial system of the Old Testament, the concept of firstfruits lives on in principle. We give the firstfruits of our paychecks to our churches as an acknowledgment that whatever money we receive for our work is a blessing from God. We give Him the first and best because, in truth, it all belongs to Him. In fact, the principle of firstfruits so permeated the thinking of early Christians that it may have been part of the reason they decided to meet on Sunday, the first day of the week.[2] By giving God the first day of the week, early Christians were acknowledging that the whole week belongs to Him.

In the same way, when you spend the first moments of your day praying, reading Scripture, and doing other activities that prime you to be productive, you are offering God the firstfruits of your day. But what exactly should you do during this time?

ELEMENTS OF A GREAT MORNING ROUTINE

In a course I teach called POWER Mornings, I suggest five basic practices that a Christian should include in his or her morning routine. Each letter of that acronym stands for one of these practices.

- **P**rayer
- **O**rganization
- **W**ord
- **E**xercise
- **R**eading & Writing

Taken together, these five rather mundane-sounding activities form a powerful foundation for a productive and God-honoring day.

Prayer & the Word: Orient Your Heart

In 2014, Navy SEAL Admiral William H. McRaven gave the commencement speech at the University of Texas. In a clip from that speech that quickly went viral, the admiral made the case for beginning your day by making the bed. He listed the many benefits of putting bed-making first in your day:

- It gives you a small sense of pride
- It encourages you to accomplish the next task of the day
- It reinforces that the little things in life matter
- And if you have a bad day, at least you can come home to a made bed

Admiral McRaven ended this part of the speech by saying, "If you want to change the world, start off by making your bed."[3]

It was quaint but practical advice, and it applies to more than just making the bed. The larger point the admiral was making was that *big change comes from simple daily habits.* When you discipline yourself to do small things over a long period of time, the results compound. Have you ever noticed that when you exercise in the morning, the rest of the day is usually more productive? That's because when we keep good habits, we are keeping promises to ourselves. Many of us carry around a mild sense of guilt because we tell ourselves we are going to practice good habits but then fail to do so. However, when we start keeping just one good habit, we begin breaking the pattern of broken promises to self and are motivated to keep the other promises we've made to ourselves also.

But Christians shouldn't start their days with just any habit. Our culture encourages early morning routines so that we can get a head start on our work and get more done. And while that may be helpful, the Christian's morning routine should not begin with speeding up to meet the workday but rather slowing down to meet with God. How you start the day sets the tone for the rest of it. And I believe the best way for Christians to begin their day is with prayer and Bible reading (right after you've made your bed of course). These are the "P" and "W" from the POWER Mornings acronym—prayer and the Word. And there are at least three good reasons to wake up early to read your Bible and pray first thing in the morning.

First, rising early to meet with God is the example we see in Scripture. This is how Jesus started His days. Mark 1:35 says, "In the early morning, while it was still dark, Jesus got up, left the house and went away to a secluded place, and was praying there" (NIV). In the busyness of ministry, the only time our Lord could find privacy, peace, and quiet was while others were still sleeping. We see a similar example echoed in the Psalms: "I rise before dawn and cry for help; I wait for Your words" (Ps. 119:147). And in Psalm 5:3, "In the morning, LORD, you hear my voice; in the morning I lay my requests before you and wait expectantly" (NIV). Saints throughout history have always made a practice of beginning their day fellowshipping with the Almighty.

> *The simple choice of picking up your Bible before you pick up your phone in the morning is a cosmic act of defiance against your own sinful heart.*

Second, beginning the day reading God's Word and praying reminds you of your purpose. The cares and troubles of this life have a way of making us myopic. The busier and more stressed we get, the more our eyes tilt downward. We forget to look at Christ and become hyper-focused on our present situation. This is a discouraging and spiritually dangerous posture. In Jesus' parable of the soils in Mark 4, He describes the thorny soil that chokes out the seed of faith as "the cares of the world" (Mark 4:19). It's important that we make a habit of lifting our eyes back to Jesus, every single day. Why not prioritize it by praying and reading the Word first thing every morning?

The third reason to begin your morning routine with prayer and Bible reading is that it sets your priorities straight.

The simple choice of picking up your Bible before you pick up your phone in the morning is a cosmic act of defiance against your own sinful heart.

When you start your morning with the news, email, or social media, you are setting the tone for the day ahead. Just as a hatchling imprints on the first face it sees, what you first engage with upon waking has an effect on the rest of your day. Put everything else on hold until you've first met with God.

It's not easy to get up early to meet with God. But it's worth it. Robert Murray M'Cheyne reflected on the importance of this simple practice in his diary: "Rose early to seek God and found Him whom my soul loveth. Who would not rise early to meet such company?"[4] Begin your mornings with God. Make prayer and the Word the first two elements of your productive morning routine.

Reading & Writing: Orient Your Mind

After orienting your heart toward God with prayer and Bible reading, now it's time to orient your mind. Mornings are wonderful for spiritual growth, but they also make a great time for intellectual and personal growth. Your productive morning routine, therefore, should also have a spot for journaling and reading.

I have kept a daily journal since I was a child. When I journal in the morning, all of the junk—the worries, the half-formed thoughts, and the cognitive detritus from yesterday—gets flushed out onto the page until my thinking runs clear. It's not the kind of writing that I'd ever want to show anyone, but that's not the point.

Writing, like speaking, is the act of forming thoughts into communicable material—something suitable to be interpreted by another mind. That's why journaling can seem strange to people who don't do it. Journaling is like talking to yourself but even weirder. But even if you don't intend for your journal to ever be read by another soul, the process of putting your thoughts into words on a page forces you to clarify your thinking. It's like starting up a lawnmower that's been sitting all winter—it might take a few pulls and it might not sound nice or smell very good, but once it finally gets started, you're ready to work. There might be some fits and starts when you first put pen to paper, but think of morning journaling as just getting your brain started.

There are also numerous spiritual benefits to daily journaling. This is why I like to journal right after I've read the Word and prayed. Journaling creates a record of God's providence in your life, something to look back on in dark days. Your journal also provides a place to record your insights from reading Scripture. In fact, one simple journaling practice I like is to choose a verse from your daily Bible reading, copy it to your journal, and write a few thoughts about it. I've found this to be a practical method for meditating on the Scriptures in a focused way.

But journaling is just one half of the "R" in a POWER morning. The other half is reading. I said earlier that successful people tend to have a morning routine, but there's another characteristic they tend to share: successful people are readers. Warren Buffet, for example, claims he read 600–1,000 pages *per day* when he was beginning his investing career. And even now, in his golden years, he says he devotes about 80 percent of his day to reading.[5]

Buffett was trying to make the most of his finances, and he recognized the importance of developing his mind to be a good investor. But every Christian has a much higher calling than temporal wealth. We've been called to steward our very lives for God. And no matter if you're a businessperson, homemaker, lineman, or line cook, you can always be honing your craft through disciplined reading.

Personally, I've found that with the busyness of life, mornings have become the best time for me to consistently get in a few pages of reading each day. You might be surprised by how much progress you can make in a year by simply reading a little bit every single day. Even if you read only three pages per day, that would add up to over 1,000 pages of reading each year. Or you could do a lot more each morning. The point isn't the volume of reading, but the consistency. A little bit each day will go a long way.

If your morning routine time is on the shorter side, consider taking advantage of audiobooks or podcasts during your commute or while exercising. Even if journaling and reading aren't your thing, you might find that other creative and mentally stimulating activities like playing music, drawing, or practicing a new skill are better for engaging your mind in the mornings. The main point of this part of the morning routine is to be setting aside a little time to train your brain to the glory of God.

Exercise: Orient Your Body

After orienting your heart through prayer and the Word and orienting your mind through journaling and reading, now it's time to orient your body to the day ahead. This is the "E" in your POWER morning. We're talking about exercise.

In the previous chapter, we looked at 1 Corinthians 6:20 and talked about the implications of being bought with a price. The principal conclusion was that your life belongs to God, but in the immediate context, the apostle Paul was specifically pointing out that our *physical bodies* are a stewardship. "Your body is a temple of the Holy Spirit" (1 Cor. 6:19). God cares about what we do with our hearts and minds, but He cares about our bodies as well.

Part of the responsibility of every Christian is to care for his or her physical body. This comes through nutrition and physical exercise. Concerning yourself with your physical body is not an unspiritual pursuit. Physical exercise, in fact, is commended by the writers of Scripture (1 Tim. 4:8). In the ancient world, unless you were outrageously wealthy, physical exercise was baked into your day-to-day life. Walking was the normal mode of transportation, and most vocations involved a lot of physical labor. In our age of cars and computers, however, most of us need to be more deliberate in stewarding our physical bodies.

The trouble is, we live in a society that idolizes physical beauty. So when we think about exercise, our minds sometimes jump to images of vain gym rats, doing three-hour workouts daily in a quest to get six-pack abs or beach bods. And not all of us have the time or inclination to be that dedicated to working out. So we figure, why bother? But exercise does not need to be an all-or-nothing endeavor. Just as Christians think about productivity differently than the world, so our motives and aims in exercise probably won't be identical to those who don't know Christ.

If your objective is merely to be a better steward of your body, then simply taking a little bit of time each day to stretch, do some pushups, or get some cardiovascular exercise in can do wonders for your energy and mental clarity for the day. Even just a twenty-minute walk each day is better than nothing. And these little steps will have tangible benefits for your overall health in the long-term. You can certainly do more than this. But my point is that for the Christian, the objective of physical exercise doesn't necessarily need to be weight loss, improved athletic performance, or getting our bodies to look a certain way. You can of course pursue those things to the glory of God, but in terms of productivity, I'm more interested in the immediate benefits of getting my heart pumping in the morning.

Regardless of what other exercise I might have planned for the day, I like to at least include some jumping jacks or pushups at the end of my morning routine. Getting my heart rate up and breaking a sweat is the last push I need to be fully awake. It also puts me in a great mood. After exercising, I feel more ready to meet the challenges of the day.

Organize: Orient Your Self to the Day

Now we come to the final letter of our POWER Mornings acronym, and that's "O" for organize. I like to save this one for last because at this point my heart, mind, and body are all oriented to the day ahead. So, naturally my mind is starting to think about the tasks I have ahead of me. Organization is the transition from my morning routine to the rest of the day. In the organize step, take five minutes to create a simple game plan for the day. Making a plan will help slingshot you into the day with all the energy, focus, and excitement that your morning routine stirred up. So don't skip this step!

This five-minute organization plan consists of just three steps.

1. Choose your most important task
2. Block out your day
3. Schedule that most important task

First, jot down the top three things you'd like to make progress on today. I like to do this on a piece of paper instead of on my phone or a computer to avoid distraction. These three things might be simple tasks like doing the laundry, getting the groceries, or paying some bills. They could also include some longer-term goals you want to move the needle on as well, like finishing that report, calling a new vendor, or writing a paper. Whatever they are, write down the top three things you'd like to work on today.

Now here's the hard part. I want you to choose *just one* of those three tasks and circle it. This doesn't mean you won't get to the other things on your list, but this one is nonnegotiable. Now decide what the next step is for that task. Often, we struggle to do our most important tasks because they are too vague. For example, if your one nonnegotiable task for today is to pay the bills, maybe the next action would be to gather all the bills at your desk. Write that down. We'll talk a lot more about clarifying and managing tasks in chapter 6, but for now, just make sure you're clear on the *one thing* you want to get done today.

Next, look at your calendar. Some people like to do this step first, but I find that looking at my calendar before I decide what's most important to work on only makes me a slave to the tyranny of the urgent. I like to decide what's most important before I see the deadlines and obligations I have today.

Now that you know what's coming up today, let's time block your day. Time blocking is a practice where you write out the hours of the day on the left side of a piece of paper. Then you literally draw blocks, or boxes, next to each hour to visually represent what you plan to do during those times. Start by drawing a block for lunch and blocks for any existing appointments from your calendar. If your job involves working in shifts, block that out as well. When you're finished, you'll have a visual representation of how much time you have available to work on today's tasks. Time blocking isn't about micromanaging your day. The purpose of it is make sure that what's most important gets prioritized, which brings us to the final step.

The third step in organizing your day is the most crucial part of this whole exercise. With things like lunch and preexisting appointments already blocked, you now need to block out a time for your single most important task. You need to force yourself to decide, right now, in advance, before the busyness of the day has a chance to crowd it out, *exactly* when you will do that one task you decided was most important. Block it out and guard that time the same way you would if it were an appointment with another person. So if you've blocked out 2 to 3 p.m. and someone asks, "Hey, are you free at 2 p.m.?" you say, "No. Sorry, I'm busy." Because you are. You have an appointment with your most important task of the day.

If you tack this simple five-minute organization plan onto the end of your morning routine, you might not feel the effects right away. But I guarantee that once you start making a daily habit of planning the day ahead, anticipating what's coming, and being deliberate about making progress on what's most important, you will start to see the productive effects compound.

That may all sound like a lot to do before breakfast, but when you measure how long each of these activities take, you can realistically do all five parts of the POWER Mornings in just thirty minutes. But however much time you designate for your morning routine, make sure you aren't giving up sleep to do it. You may feel productive in the short term, but if you're consistently forgoing sleep to wake up earlier, it will eventually catch up with you. So how do you get up earlier? Go to sleep earlier. It's that simple. Yes, this is a sacrifice, but I can tell you from personal experience that it's absolutely worth it.

Imagine what kind of person you would be in a year if you gave a portion of every single day to the Word and prayer, journaling and constructive reading, some light exercise, and deliberately planning your day around your most important tasks. Imagine how your relationship with the Lord would deepen. Imagine how sharp your thinking would become. Imagine how much better you'd feel. Give POWER Mornings a try and see how much more productive it makes you.

But we aren't trying to be productive merely for productivity's sake. Next, let's turn to the second pillar of Christian productivity: purpose.

3

PILLAR 2

THE PURPOSE OF PRODUCTIVITY

You Exist to Glorify God

—— — — ——

They say you should never go to the grocery store hungry.

Like many college freshmen, I overdid it with my newfound freedom. Finally out on my own, it was time to live life my way. But the typical lures of college life and its lack of accountability were not what animated me. I was just excited to buy whatever I wanted at the grocery store.

My problem, however, was that I didn't put much forethought into my shopping trips. Grocery list? Who needs one? My shopping strategy was to put it off until the very moment I would open the refrigerator, hungry for lunch, only to find there was nothing left to eat. Then, like a half-starved beast on the savanna, I would stagger to the grocery store in search of prey. Once there, I'd hunch over my shopping cart and careen up and down the snack food aisles, the squeaky wheels of the cart harmonizing with the rumbling in my stomach. I'd indiscriminately shovel into my cart whatever caught my

41

famished eyes. And let's just say it wasn't kale and quinoa I brought to the checkout. Cookies, cheese crackers, and ice cream were all part of this college student's complete breakfast. If it was processed and pre-packaged, it was coming with me. After checking out, I'd rush home and tear into my quarry until my stomach rumblings were exchanged for a tummy ache.

Why did I repeat this foolish quest multiple times per week in my first semester of college? You could simply chalk it up to teenage stupidity. But at its core, my habit was simply the result of not having a plan. Without a grocery list, budget, or diet to guide my food decisions, I simply followed the path of least resistance. Since I didn't plan with the end in mind, I did whatever felt right in the moment. The results of this haphazard approach to grocery shopping were, unsurprisingly, an empty wallet and the "freshman fifteen."

I like to think I'm a more disciplined grocery shopper these days (though my wife may disagree). But what I've realized is that my approach to food procurement was simply a microcosm of how I approached all of life. It was the same reason I wasn't fruitful in my studies or my work. I didn't have a plan or a purpose. Sadly, many Christians wander through life the same way I wandered through my local Kroger. We are often aimless, groping at the same wood, hay, and stubble our unsaved peers seem to be after. We've trusted Christ, we're going to church, but what exactly are we supposed to be doing with these lives while we wait for our heavenly home? What should our plan be?

PLANS COME FROM PURPOSE

Most of us know how important it is to have something to aim at when it comes to our career and personal aspirations. We have projects, set deadlines, and make goals. Maybe you want to close that account, finish that design, or lose ten pounds. Goals are great, and we'll have a lot more to say about goal setting in chapter 8. But we need to start with a more fundamental question: Why? Why am I here? What is the higher purpose of all my goals? What binds them together? If we want to redeem productivity, we have to understand why we are here and what it is we are supposed to be accomplishing with these lives. If the origin of our productivity has to do with whose we are, purpose has to do with where it's all going. What's the ultimate point of being productive?

Secular approaches to productivity contain valuable strategies that can help us make effective plans for achieving our goals. For example, I'll be forever thankful for David Allen's book *Getting Things Done*. The methodology it espouses has radically changed how I manage my tasks and projects (we'll talk more about task management in chapter 6, by the way). But while these strategies might be able to help you reach your goals, no productivity expert can tell you *what* your ultimate goal should be. The answer to that question must come from God.

If your favorite self-development guru is not a believer in Jesus Christ, then he or she does not share the same ultimate life goal as you. If we uncritically apply everything these experts say, we'll find ourselves adopting more than just their systems—we'll adopt their values. We might get a lot more things done along the way, but the destination will not be where Christ would have us go. Christians have a different value system from the world; we have a different purpose. And that should change how we approach everything in life, including our productivity.

WHY WE'RE HERE

As we saw in the first pillar, thoughtful reflection on personal productivity will always lead you to ask higher level questions. The secular productivity experts know this too. David Allen writes, "At the topmost level of thinking you'll need to ask some of the ultimate questions: Why does your company exist? Why do you exist? What is the core DNA of your existence, personally and/or organizationally, that drives your choices?"[1] We often assign subjects like time management and goal setting to the "practical" category of our thinking. But here's David Allen, *the* to-do list guy, insisting that in order to be productive you have to answer one of life's deepest philosophical questions: Why am I here? The problem with secular works on productivity isn't that they don't talk about life's ultimate goal. The problem is that they do, and they're wrong about it.

Allen, of course, isn't the only one blending productivity and philosophy. Stephen Covey is one of the godfathers of the time management movement. His book *The 7 Habits of Highly Effective People*[2] and his FranklinCovey planners have become standard bookshelf candy in the offices of businesspeople around the world. And Covey understood that purpose cannot be disconnected from productivity.

In *First Things First*, a book Covey helped write in 1994, he says there have been four generations of time management systems.[3] The first generation simply focused on organization. It dealt with things like to-do lists and work environment. The second generation put a greater focus on time and the future. Tools like goal setting and calendars joined the daily to-do list as standard weapons in the productivity arsenal. In the third generation, productivity systems began to emphasize the role of personal values. They emphasized the importance of identifying your own values and planning your goals accordingly. The fourth generation of personal productivity, and the one which Covey advocates for in *First Things First*, is an approach that combines personal values with transcendent principles. He emphasizes that while personal values are subjective and may change with time, principles are objective and unchanging. These principles include things like justice, fairness, and truth. Covey calls this fourth generation of time management "principle-centered" leadership.

This progression makes me wonder if the fifth generation of time management will add a deity and a holy book. Because when you get to transcendent principles, you aren't talking about productivity anymore, you're talking about religion. You have to get those transcendent principles from somewhere. Covey, a member of the Church of Jesus Christ of Latter-day Saints, got those principles from his religion. He authored several devotional works for Mormons, including a book released in 1982 titled *The Divine Center*. In that book, written to a Mormon audience, he explains how he teaches LDS principles by couching them in different language.[4]

> *Productivity flows from purpose. Without knowing who you are and why you're here, there will be no controlling purpose that unites your productive efforts, no chief end to all of that toil.*

I'm not trying to pick on Allen and Covey. They are simply saying the quiet part out loud. It's an undeniable truth—when you follow the path of personal productivity to its logical conclusion, you always end at religion. Since man was made to find meaning in his work, productivity and purpose are inextricable. So, as much as I value their methods, I'm not interested in the religious philosophy of secular productivity experts. But I can't fault them for trying to address the big questions of life.

Productivity flows from purpose. Without knowing who you are and why you're here, there will be no controlling purpose that unites your productive efforts, no chief end to all of that toil.

This is precisely why productivity needs redeeming. Christians have answers to these ultimate questions. We have been redeemed for a very specific purpose: to glorify God. And that ought to change everything about how we approach our work.

GLORY IS THE GOAL

What is the Christian's ultimate goal? The ultimate goal, or "the chief end of man," as the Westminster Shorter Catechism puts it, is to "glorify God and enjoy Him forever."[5] You were created to glorify God (Isa. 43:7). And if you are in Christ, you were saved to glorify God (Rom. 15:7), given work to glorify God (Eph. 2:10), and you will someday be resurrected unto eternal life to glorify God forever (Rev. 5:13). God's glory is our goal, our reason for existing. It's why we're here. We were made to be productive as we find our purpose in glorifying God in our labors. But what does it mean to glorify God?

Terms like "glory" and "glorify" are so common in Christian circles that we sometimes don't pause to understand what they mean. Stop reading for a second and see if you can define the word glory in a sentence or two.

Harder than it sounds, right?

That we would be comfortable with such an imprecise definition is astounding when you consider the Bible uses the word glory over 400 times![6] If we want to understand our chief purpose in life and have the kind of productivity that flows from it, we must begin by understanding exactly what it means to glorify God.

HOW WE GLORIFY

Traditionally, theologians have spoken about God's glory in two categories: His intrinsic glory and His ascribed glory. God's intrinsic glory is that which He has in Himself. It is not an attribute of God but rather the visible manifestation of all He is. Biblical synonyms for glory are usually words having to do with light. They include terms like splendor or brightness. We don't call glory an attribute of God because it was often seen by the saints of old, whereas God Himself is invisible (1 Tim. 1:17).[7]

Here's a helpful way to think about it: As the sun has light, so God has glory. The light of the sun is not the sun, yet it would not be the sun if it did not give forth light. In the same way, the glory of God is not God, yet He would not be God if He did not manifest glory. As Thomas Watson put it, "Glory is the sparkling of Deity."[8]

But when we speak of humans glorifying God, we are not suggesting that we are somehow adding to that intrinsic glory. That would be blasphemous. God's glory cannot receive any addition because it is perfect, and it cannot diminish because God is unchanging and will not allow His glory to be given away (Isa. 48:11). So, if I can't add to God's glory, in what sense can I, a sinful creature, be said to "glorify God?" This brings us to God's ascribed glory.

First Chronicles 16:28–29 declares:

> Ascribe to the LORD, O families of the peoples,
> ascribe to the LORD glory and strength!
> Ascribe to the LORD the glory due his name;
> bring an offering and come before him!
> Worship the LORD in the splendor of holiness.

When we talk about glorifying God, what we really mean is ascribing glory to Him. Glorifying God is regarding Him as worthy of praise. That 1 Chronicles passage refers to glorifying God in the context of the invitation to praise and worship Him. And glorifying God with our words is a big part of how we ascribe Him glory. But we are also to glorify Him with what we do: "So, whether you eat or drink, or whatever you do, do all to the glory of God" (1 Cor. 10:31). To glorify God means that through word, deed, and attitude, both publicly and privately, I magnify God as worthy of praise, adoration, and service. Again, Watson captures it well: "The glory we give God is nothing else but our lifting up his name in the world, and magnifying him in the eyes of others."[9]

When we speak of ascribing glory to God, or glorifying God, we are just talking about pointing. My life, my work, and my thoughts are to be one giant arrow that reads "worthy" and points to God. If God is the sun and glory is His light, then we are the moon, reflecting God's glory for all to see. It is not our own glory but His that we show forth to the world. In fact, Jesus says something very similar to this in Matthew 5:16: "In the same way, let your light shine before others, so that they may see your good works and give glory to your Father who is in heaven." We shine with good works, not that we would be glorified, but that others, upon seeing our good works, would turn and praise the source of that light, the One who wrought those good works in us. We'll talk more about how good works factor into our productivity in chapter 5.

GLORIFYING GOD THROUGH PRODUCTIVITY

When my wife and I first moved to Los Angeles, we didn't have much money. So we used Craigslist to find cheap secondhand furniture. This worked out well for our budget, and it also provided an interesting glimpse into life in LA.

LA has rightly earned a reputation of being a place where people go to chase dreams of fame and glory. It's the land of Hollywood, and it draws aspiring actors like moths to a flame. While auditioning and waiting for their big break, however, these aspiring actors still have bills to pay. Kim and I learned that aspiring actors always call themselves actors, no matter what their day job is and even if they've never acted a day in their lives.

It was the same story every time. We would drive to someone's home to pick up a couch or chair. Naturally, before the exchange, we'd have some small talk with the seller. And without fail, when we'd ask the question, "So what do you do?" we'd get some version of the same answer. Everyone in LA is a "something slash actor." We met a DJ/Actor, a Panera Bread Baker/Actor, and even an Elementary Math Teacher/Actor. It was so common that we made a game out of guessing "what-slash-actor" the seller would be when we pulled up to his or her home. But it reminded me of someone else who had two seemingly incongruous job titles.

Abraham Kuyper was also a man whose career was defined by two professions. Kuyper was a Dutch theologian who also happened to be the prime minister of the Netherlands in the early 1900s. To our ears, politician/theologian might sound as odd a juxtaposition as plumber/actor. But for Kuyper it made perfect sense. He understood that what we believe about God should permeate every area of our lives, including our work. Since we have been called to this high purpose of glorifying God, it makes sense that our work would be the main vehicle for accomplishing these ends.

When Kuyper went into politics, he brought his theology with him. In truth, we all do this. Our beliefs about God, mankind, and ourselves will come out in every area of life, including our work and productivity. But a productive Christian will consciously make the connection between work and the purpose of glorifying God. Kuyper said, "Whatever man may stand, whatever he may do, to whatever he may apply his hand—in agriculture, in commerce, and in industry, or his mind, in the world of art, and science—he is, in whatsoever it may be, constantly standing before the face of God. And above all, he has to aim at the glory of his God."[10]

Whatever your life's calling, you will always be that-thing-slash-God-glorifier. You might be a mother-slash-God-glorifier, CEO-slash-God-glorifier, student-slash-God-glorifier, or marketer-slash-God-glorifier. What you do is not your purpose, it's how you fulfill your ultimate purpose. Your purpose isn't to be productive; it is to bring God glory through all that you do. But with such an important mission, you will naturally seek to be productive in your calling. That's what good stewards do. As Thomas Watson put it, "The glory of God is a silver thread which must run through all our actions."[11] Knowing we have such an important purpose can be intimidating. We may even be tempted to see it as a burden, but it is just the opposite.

THE PRIVILEGE OF PURPOSE

When I was five years old, my dad took his own life, leaving me, my mom, and my two siblings confused and fatherless. My mother never remarried, so I grew up without a father in my life. We know statistically that kids who grow up without a dad are more likely to become involved in illicit activities like crime or drugs. By God's grace, thankfully, I didn't get into those things myself, but I understand why some do. Growing up without a dad is confusing. So much of our identity is tied up in what our parents model for us and affirm in us. When you don't have someone showing you what it looks like to walk out your purpose, you will naturally be confused about your place in this world.

As I entered my teen years, I remember how aimless I was. While my friends looked toward their futures, seeming so confident in where they were going, I felt like I didn't even know *who* I was, much less *what* I was supposed to be doing. I looked to anyone who would give me some clear direction. This, I believe, is why some fatherless kids join gangs (or cults for that matter). There is something so clarifying about someone sitting you down and saying, "This is who you are. You are one of us. And this is what we're about." We crave that kind of clarity because we all want to know what our purpose is.

Regardless of how you grew up, I'm guessing you've known the pain of purposelessness. Most people spend their whole lives wandering the grocery store aisles of life wondering, "Why am I here? What's my purpose?" Many don't have a plan because they don't know why they're here. But Christians have a straightforward, no-nonsense target drawn with bold lines and bright colors. You are here to glorify God. And having this clear purpose is an amazing gift from God! Christians have the privilege of purpose. Don't waste it.

For me, discovering that the God who is the "Father of the fatherless" (Ps. 68:5) had given *me* a purpose was completely life-changing. As I started to understand what it meant to lead a God-glorifying life, all the clouds of confusion began to clear. Slowly, I stopped feeling so much like that confused, fatherless boy and instead began to feel like a man with a mission from my heavenly Father. God not only saved me from my sins, He gave me a purpose. And by His grace I want to fulfill that purpose well, making the most of this life for His glory.

When we embrace our purpose in this world, it has a tremendous focusing effect on all that we do. The world will say we are here to make ourselves happy, rich, and successful. But all of these purposes fall short of our true and ultimate purpose: we exist to glorify God.

But the enemy of purpose is confusion. There are so many ways we can be distracted from that mission. Even if we know our purpose is to glorify God, it's easy to forget for a season, especially when we get busy. So in the next chapter we'll talk about some practical ways to organize your life to avoid distraction. Because purposeful productivity begins with focus, and to be focused we need to get organized.

4

PRACTICE 2

GET ORGANIZED

Clarifying the first two pillars of productivity—that you belong to God and that your purpose in life is to bring Him glory—is exciting. You know who you are and why you are here. Knowing these truths helps you wake up each day with a sense of mission for your work, your home life, and even your hobbies. But distraction is the great enemy of a purposeful life. And our world is full of distractions. From news to social media to gossip to Netflix, there are a million things vying for our attention each day. And each of these distractions carries its own implicit message about who you are and why you are here. But it is possible, even in this age of distraction, for productive Christians to stay focused on what matters most.

How many mornings have you woken up, ready to meet the day, only to roll over and see your phone begging you to check something really quick? Before your day has even begun, you're already distracted. That clear sense of purpose you awoke with has been enveloped by a fog of anxiety-inducing noise. And that's just the morning. All throughout our day we are bombarded with interruptions, obstructions, and diversions that beg us to do something, anything, other than what we set out to do. We all know lack of focus is a problem. Nevertheless, most of us go about fighting distraction in exactly the wrong way.

Most people think the key to fighting distraction is willpower. We think if we just grit our teeth and muster up some stoic self-discipline, then we can block out the noise. The better path to focus, however, is to not allow yourself to be distracted in the first place. How do you do that? You get organized.

OPTIMIZING YOUR ENVIRONMENT

Certainly, there are times when we simply must force ourselves to block out the noise and get our work done. If you work in an office with an open floor plan, have a house full of kids, or are reading in a coffee shop, it will require willpower to maintain your focus. But as much as possible, we should seek to optimize our environments so that we have fewer distractions fighting for our attention. The less we need to rely on willpower to stay focused, the better. Researcher and writer Sönke Ahrens notes, "Studies on highly successful people have proven again and again that success is not the result of strong willpower and the ability to overcome resistance, but rather the result of smart working environments that avoid resistance in the first place."[1] The apostle Paul put it more succinctly: flee temptation (see Rom. 13:14; 1 Cor. 6:18; 2 Tim. 2:22).

Now, I'm not suggesting that every temptation to distraction is a temptation to sin, but the same principle that guides how we react to opportunities to indulge the flesh can be applied when our notifications are begging us to check Instagram. Whether it's a sinful temptation or not, the best way to fight isn't through testing your willpower, it's by putting the temptation out of reach. It's as true for your personal holiness as it is for your self-discipline—flee temptation. The principle is simple: change your environment so that good habits are easier and bad habits are harder. James Clear, in his book *Atomic Habits*, writes, "Environment is the invisible hand that shapes human behavior."[2]

If you've ever gone on a diet, you know that the worst thing you can do is keep your favorite snack foods in the house. It's the same with distraction. If you really want to live a focused and productive life for God's glory, you've got to put the things that tempt you to distraction far out of reach. But the reason we often fail to do this obvious thing is because it takes planning. It takes being organized. And the results of being organized are not always felt immediately.

GROWTH THROUGH ORDER

When I was working from home at the start of the COVID-19 pandemic, I, like many people, tried my hand at gardening. I had never grown anything before (aside from maybe the odd patch of mold on food I'd left in the fridge too long). But I learned a lot about gardening in 2020. I grew tomatoes, beets, and a variety of herbs. Going into it, I knew that gardening would require patience, time, and consistent attention, but I was surprised to discover just how much organization was required.

To grow a successful garden, there are many factors you need to track. You must plant at the right times, make sure your soil is healthy, water the right amount at the right intervals, fertilize, weed, prune, and much more. Even with my small garden, I found that I needed to keep careful notes about those details because I would quickly forget what I'd done to which plants and when. When I wasn't organized, the plants suffered and I had a less productive yield. I learned that a disorganized garden is an unsuccessful garden.

Personal growth is like a garden. When we carefully cultivate environments that make it easier to do the right things, and harder to do the wrong things, we experience growth. This is true with regard to our spiritual growth as we organize so that we are consistently benefiting from the means of grace. But it's true of personal growth as well. When we keep our environments orderly, we grow.

IN THE IMAGE OF AN ORDERLY GOD

There's something so nice about sitting down at an organized desk. Having everything in its proper place promotes hard work, clear thinking, and a sense of peace. Though it can often be easier to live in a state of disorderliness, no one really enjoys it. Even the messiest among us desire to live a more orderly life. We are drawn to orderliness because God is a God of order, and we were created in His image.

When the apostle Paul wrote his first letter to the church in Corinth, he addressed some serious problems. One of those problems was that their church services were completely out of control. Things were so wild that Paul was legitimately concerned that outsiders would come and think the Corinthian Christians were insane (1 Cor. 14:23). Paul gave them specific instructions for how to quell some of the chaos that was happening in their services, but in doing so he appealed to a broader principle: God is a God of order. "For God is not a God of confusion but of peace" (1 Cor. 14:33). And we can draw applications from this principle about how we approach other areas of life, including our productivity.

Everywhere you look in this world you see the fingerprints of God's orderliness. We see it in creation's structures and dependable rhythms. The sun rises and sets, the seasons change every year, and gravity works the same on Tuesday as it does on Saturday. This is all because an orderly God made things that way (Gen. 1:14–18, 31; Ps. 104:19). This world, tainted as it may be by the curse, is still so well ordered that the biblical writers even use its unchanging dependability to illustrate how we can depend on God's faithfulness to His promises: "Let us know; let us press on to know the LORD; his going out is sure as the dawn; he will come to us as the showers, as the spring rains that water the earth" (Hos. 6:3).

But because the world is indeed under a curse, we do not see that orderliness everywhere. If left unattended, gardens become overgrown or eaten up by pests. And it's the same with our lives. Entropy never takes a day off. The dishes in your kitchen sink will attest to that. The only way to fight back against the slow creep of chaos is to vigilantly lead orderly lives. Doing so honors the orderly God in whose image we were made, it ensures we are maturing, and it results in long-lasting fruitfulness. To be productive, you need to get organized. But where to begin?

ORGANIZE THESE THREE ENVIRONMENTS FIRST

I'm no Marie Kondo. I'm not going to tell you how to fold your underwear or suggest you should talk to your stuff before you throw it in the trash. In fact, to be honest with you, I'm not naturally a very tidy person myself. But I want to make the most of this life, so I try to be organized where it counts. And I've found that there are three specific environments that give me the most productivity bang for my organizing buck. By organizing your bedroom, your morning routine space, and your work area, you will experience outsized productivity results.

Your Bedroom

The bedroom might seem like an odd place to start when talking about organizing for productivity. But we already talked about the productive value of a morning routine, and a great morning begins with a great night's sleep. Here are a few simple ways you can prepare your bedroom to make it easier to get the best sleep you can.

First, get blackout curtains. Having the room totally dark signals to your body that it's time to go to sleep and stay asleep. Second, eliminate noise. If you can't get total quiet in your bedroom, consider getting some ear plugs or a white noise machine. These are small things, but do them and you'll soon observe the trickle effect of how a good night's sleep improves your productivity.

After managing the light and noise in your bedroom, look at your bedside table. One of the most important things you can do is *not* keep your phone beside your bed. But almost everyone does this. We've all sat in bed in the morning way longer than we planned to because we started reading the news or checking our email the moment we woke up. Then we begin the day in an anxious brain fog. Why not charge your phone across the room instead? Or better yet, in another room entirely. A phone is the worst thing you can keep on your bedside table.

Researcher Anne-Laure Le Cunff argues that you should keep just three sets of items on your bedside table.[3]

- Pen and paper
- Book and lamp
- Alarm clock

The pen and paper allow you to journal or jot down stray thoughts before bed or upon waking. The book and lamp allow you to wind down with analog reading and avoid the blue light of your phone, which has been shown to suppress melatonin levels, thus disrupting your body's ability to make you feel sleepy. A physical book also helps you avoid the endless buffet of information nuggets presented by the internet. And a good old-fashioned alarm clock allows you to wake up on time without depending on your phone.

Your Morning Routine Space

God created us as integrated beings, soul and body. Therefore, our physical environments have tremendous influence on our emotions and thoughts. When we first wake up, even the smallest thing can discourage us from going through with our morning routine. This is why people often recommend that if you plan to go to the gym in the morning, you should set out your shoes and gym clothes the night before. Remove as much friction as possible from the good habits you want to form. The same applies to your morning routine space.

To borrow a friend's joke, imagine how bad you'd be at brushing your teeth if you kept your toothbrush in the garage. Would you consistently brush your teeth if every time you went to brush you had to tromp out to the garage, bring the toothbrush to the bathroom, brush, and go back out and put it away next to the weed whacker? Brushing our teeth is an easy habit because the toothbrush is right there next to the sink. We can make other habits easier by the same principle.

Keep your space clean. Nothing makes me want to sit down and read my Bible less than when everything is a mess, or worse, when I can't even find my Bible! Pick up your morning routine area and reset it at the end of each morning. Fold your blanket, put the pillows back on the couch, stack your Bible and notebook, and make it tidy and inviting for tomorrow.

Make your space smell nice. God has made us so that our memories are tied strongly to our sense of smell. If you've ever caught a whiff of a charcoal fire and been instantly transported back to a summer barbecue, or if you've detected the scent of pine needles on a fall breeze and found yourself reminiscing about a camping trip, you know what I'm talking about. Try to leverage the incredible power of smell to create a positive memory about your morning routine space. Make a habit of using a specific scented candle or diffuse some essential oils, whatever it takes. After you do this a few times, your mind will develop a positive association with that scent, and you'll more easily slip into morning routine mode when you smell it.

Keep your plan visible. I like to have a physical, printed plan for my morning routine and Bible reading, which helps in a couple of ways. First, it keeps me off my distracting electronic devices. I love my Bible apps, but I never use them for my Bible reading plan. It's just too tempting to go to another app and get distracted. Second, a printed plan keeps each step of your routine visible. I know exactly what to do next in my morning routine without having to think. Keeping your plans visible is a great way to make any habit more likely to succeed.

Your Work Area

What constitutes your work area will differ depending on your calling. It may be your desk, the back of your truck, your computer's file system, or it may literally be your kitchen. The point is, if you want to steward your work well for God's glory, you need to keep your knives sharp and your ingredients at the ready. Here are three practices that can be helpful for getting any work area organized and ready for use.

First, purge the unnecessary. If your space is out of control, you don't just need to tidy up, you need to take radical action. Block off an hour or two. Depending on the size of your workspace this might require even more time. Start by clearing a big area and making two piles: "Keep" and "Go." Now go through *everything*, placing items into the two piles as you go. Be ruthless. Part of the objective in this first phase is simply to take stock of everything you have. When you're done, your drawers, cabinets, or whatever storage areas you use in your workspace should be empty. And you should have two huge piles.

Second, have a place for everything. Now that you know what you want to keep, make sure there's a place for all of it. Depending on your situation, you might already have places for each thing, but this is still a good chance to reevaluate how you organize your stuff. And if you don't already have designated homes for your different items, now is the time to figure that out. Start by dividing your "keep" pile into categories. You can use Tim Challies's simple organizing principle, "a home for everything, and like goes with like."[4] In my office, I have drawers for things like stationery, camera gear, and reference materials. Once you have your smaller piles, store them in a logical way. Put the things you use most frequently closer to the center of your work area. Less frequently used items can be stored in more difficult to access spaces—the back of drawers, top of the closet, etc. Now, hopefully, your work area is starting to feel more functional. But if you don't watch out, disorganization will quickly reenter the picture.

Third, schedule a weekly tidy up. The best way I've found for staving off the unwinding of my organization is to not reserve organizing only for the annual spring cleaning. Dedicate a few minutes each week to putting things back in order, and you won't have to do a giant half-day purge quite as often. For me, Friday afternoon is the time I review my projects, clean out my inboxes, and organize my desk. I try not to schedule meetings between 3:30 and 5:00 p.m. on Friday. I keep it booked for my weekly review and tidy up. When I'm faithful to this weekly routine, my work area stays clear and consequently so does my mind.

When we organize our physical world, it has a clarifying effect on our mental and spiritual worlds as well. If you want to play the game of productivity on hard mode, then stay disorganized. But if you want to optimize your life so you can be as faithful of a steward as possible, then organize your environments. Start with your bedroom, morning routine space, and work area. And just watch how the God of order uses the means of your organized environments to enable your God-glorifying productive efforts.

5

8

PILLAR 3

THE CONTENT OF PRODUCTIVITY

You Were Saved to Bear Fruit for God

—— – – ——

Imagine two men working for the same company in the same position. They have the exact same job description and the same list of duties. They are also equally good at their job, scoring the same on their performance reviews each quarter. Yet one of them is a Christian and the other is not. By all external measures, they appear to be equally productive. Yet, when considered according to God's standards, the Christian is orders of magnitude more productive than the nonbeliever. How can I say that? Because Christians measure our productivity differently than the world. To redeem productivity, we need to stop judging our productivity the same way the world does. And that begins by redeeming the content of productivity.

Christians were saved not just to get more things done, but to bear fruit for God.

In any industry, productivity is typically judged purely on what we might call practical effectiveness. Did you get the job done and get

3

it done well? Were you efficient and effective? Did you increase the bottom line? This same pragmatic understanding of productivity can show up in our homes as well. Did you get all the laundry done? Did the kids get bathed? Are the bills paid? Good. You were productive this week. It can even appear in our churches when we start measuring effectiveness by external outcomes. Is the number of people in our church growing? Did we get good feedback on the worship music this week? Is giving up or down? These practical concerns are not unimportant. Nevertheless, be it in our jobs, homes, or churches, practical effectiveness is never the true measure of a Christian's productivity. It is only the byproduct. God judges the content of our productivity in a more holistic manner.

THE LAYERS OF CHRISTIAN PRODUCTIVITY

The content of Christian productivity consists of three layers.

- Internal character
- External obedience
- Practical effectiveness

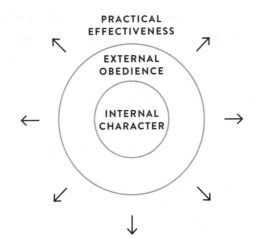

These make up the why, how, and what of the content of God-honoring productivity. As we are transformed by Christ, there should be a natural progression from our internal character to external obedience to His commands. A byproduct of these two is practical effectiveness in our work. In other words, what the world thinks of as the content of productivity is only the tip of the iceberg—there is much more going on below the surface. And when

> *God will judge your productivity not just by the what but also by the why and how.*

we try to jump straight to practical effectiveness, skipping over internal character and external obedience, what we have is not God-honoring productivity but hypocrisy.

When the world talks about the content of productivity, it only includes practical effectiveness. "I'm good at my job because I get a lot done." That's how your employer will judge your productivity. But, as I've emphasized throughout this book, God will judge your productivity not just by the *what* but also by the *why* and *how*. Sure, you got a lot done, but amid that work was your heart characterized by attitudes and motives that are honoring to God? Were you obedient to God when opportunities arose? If you have internal character and external obedience, practical effectiveness often follows naturally. You will tend to be good at your job in the practical sense. But if you only focus on practical effectiveness, you end up with a pragmatic, hollow sort of productivity that does not serve to glorify God.

Take the issue of integrity for example. The nonbeliever may have integrity at work because he understands that you never know when someone might be watching. So it's best to not cut corners or lie even if you think you won't get caught. And sure, even wrongly motivated integrity has its rewards. He will probably have more long-term business relationships because people know they can trust him, and he will have less stress from trying to manage lies. But this is only pragmatic integrity. It's not rooted in internal character. The Christian has integrity not because it's good business sense but because he serves a God of truth and wants to honor Him by being a man of truth. The Christian woman has integrity because she loves her neighbor and does not wish to defraud or deceive him. This internal character of truthfulness comes out in the practical obedience of honesty, and it results in the practical effectiveness of neighbors, colleagues, and clients who trust us. They believe we have their best interests at heart because we truly do.

If these two approaches to integrity have the same result, why does it matter whether a person's practical effectiveness is rooted in internal character and practical obedience? Because Christians are not merely concerned with the temporal results of our productivity. We recognize that productivity itself is a vehicle for honoring God. We also recognize that the entire content of our productivity—the how, why, and the what—will be judged by God. In chapter 9, we will talk more about how this expectation of judgment forms the greatest motivation to productivity.

Productivity gurus often emphasize the importance of character in our work and productivity. But if they don't believe the Bible, they have nowhere to ground that value. So they appeal to pragmatic arguments like we saw with integrity. Jon Huntsman Sr., for example, is a multi-billionaire who started a chemical company and grew it to $12 billion. In his book *Winners Never Cheat*, he explains the practical benefits of honesty in business: "There are, basically, three kinds of people: the unsuccessful, the temporarily successful, and those who become and remain successful. The difference is character."[1] The message is this: if you want to succeed, have character. If you're honest, you'll do more deals, make more money, and people will like you more. And, in part, those who argue this way are right! It is wise to walk in an upright manner. And such a walk tends to lead to positive temporal results. Similar sentiments about the value of wisdom are echoed in the Proverbs. But as an ultimate motivation for having good character, this is a sad, utilitarian way to think about character.

This pragmatic view of character's role in productivity comes in part from the language we use when we talk about productivity. Modern personal productivity is typically viewed through the metaphor of factories and machines, while the Bible talks about productivity using organic metaphors. The former defaults to bottom-line thinking that leads to pragmatism; the latter produces a holistic view of our work and an understanding of how the whole person honors God through his or her productivity, whether or not he or she is being practically effective.

FROM THE FACTORY FLOOR TO THE DESK CHAIR

Who doesn't love a good metaphor? Metaphors add romance to our language, like when Romeo describes Juliet's beauty, "But soft, what light through yonder window breaks? It is the east and Juliet is the sun." Metaphors add humor, like when a teacher refers to the wild behavior of her students by calling the classroom a zoo. The power of metaphor is that it allows us to visualize abstract concepts and thus make them more memorable. Jesus was fond of using metaphors for this purpose as well, calling Himself "the bread of life" and His followers "the salt of the earth" (John 6:35; Matt. 5:13). These metaphors stick with us because they invoke vivid images for us to attach concepts to. Like bread, Jesus sustains. Like salt, Christians preserve and add flavor to the world. A simple metaphor can pack a lot of meaning into a few memorable words.

Because of their power to influence how we think and feel about things, the metaphors we use to talk about a topic are very important. In our mission to redeem productivity, we must take care not to undiscerningly accept the definitions the world uses for productivity. But perhaps even more importantly, we should be wary of borrowing unbiblical metaphors for productivity as well, because these metaphors will shape our thinking.

If you listen closely to the language we use to talk about productivity and time management, you'll notice a pattern. We speak about productivity in almost exclusively mechanical terms. We talk about the way humans work using the language of factories and machines. We'll use words like "efficiency" and "output" and expressions such as "running like a well-oiled machine." Now that computers are so prevalent, we've extended our mechanical metaphors to include them as well, referring to our brains as a hard drive or speaking of our working capacity as bandwidth. In fact, I've probably already done it several times in this book.

Even when we talk about biblical passages that touch on productivity, we often import mechanical imagery that would have been foreign to the biblical author. Ephesians 5:15–16 is a popular passage Christians use to talk about time management and the importance of "redeeming the time" (KJV). We hear those words and instinctively picture a clock. We start thinking of how we can make sure we don't waste a single moment of time. But Paul wasn't thinking about his wristwatch. He didn't have a wristwatch. The mechanical clock had yet to be invented, and as such the ancient world thought about time much differently than we do today.[2] The phrase rendered "redeeming the time" in the King James Bible is more about making the most of opportunities or seasons, not hours. It's a subtle but significant difference. The fact that we skip right over what Paul meant is a testament to just how much of our thinking about work has been shaped by the Industrial Revolution and its mechanical view of productivity.

When I first got into the world of personal productivity, this is exactly how I started to think of myself—like a machine. I needed to optimize every moment of the day for maximum efficiency. Because of this, I didn't account for things like varying energy levels, cycles of focus, my mood, or even my own need for rest. I pushed myself to the extreme and, no surprise, I burned out (yes, burnout is another mechanical metaphor). I forgot that I was a man, not a machine. Humans aren't productive in the same way machines are. That sounds obvious, so why do we so often talk about human productivity as if we are machines? Why are our metaphors so mechanical? I believe the answer is found in part in the history of the productivity movement.

Modern theories of personal productivity are rooted in principles of factory management developed during the Industrial Revolution. The beginnings of the productivity movement can be traced to Frederick Winslow Taylor, a mechanical engineer who developed methods for improving industrial efficiency. His 1911 book, *The Principles of Scientific Management,* became required reading for anyone who wanted their factory to be more competitive. Later, Peter Drucker adapted and expanded upon Taylor's theories and applied them to the white-collar business world. The personal productivity movement was born. Anyone writing on productivity today is an ideological descendant of Taylor and Drucker, whether he or she is aware of it or not. Yet even though today's productivity literature is almost exclusively concerned with the domain of knowledge workers, we still tend to think and speak about productivity using Taylor's mechanical terms. And I'm convinced it's this mechanical view of productivity, which treats people like machines and is only concerned with increasing efficiency, that has led to the meaninglessness, lack of satisfaction, and

We are called to be productive like a tree, not an assembly line.

desperate I-can-never-catch-up sense so many people feel regarding their work. Instead of helping solve these issues, the mechanical view of human productivity only makes them worse. Part of the reason you feel like you are on a treadmill you can't get off is because you have bought into mechanical metaphors for personal productivity and their unrealistic expectations.

The good news is that the Bible does not speak about productivity in mechanical terms. Instead, it uses organic metaphors.

We are called to be productive like a tree, not an assembly line.

I believe this seemingly insignificant difference in metaphor will change the way you think about the content of your personal productivity forever. When you embrace the organic view of personal productivity, you are able accomplish more of what really matters, feel less frenzied, and produce work in a much more God-honoring way. God has designed us for fruitfulness.

PRODUCTIVITY IS FRUITFULNESS

Have you ever noticed that fruits and vegetables are found in the "produce" section of the grocery store? That's because long before productivity was a way of talking about how many cars Henry Ford's assembly lines could turn out, the number of deals a salesman closed, or how many lines of code a computer programmer could write in a day, it referred to crop yield. A productive apple tree is one that bears a lot of apples. And this organic view is exactly how the Bible talks about our productivity.

From the beginning, mankind was called to fruitfulness. "And God blessed them. And God said to them, 'Be fruitful and multiply and fill the earth and subdue it, and have dominion over the fish of the sea and over the birds of the heavens and over every living thing that moves on the earth'" (Gen. 1:28). Fruitful labor is in our DNA. Man was made for this kind of productivity.

Once you notice the connection between fruit and productivity, suddenly you start to see just how much the Bible has to say on the topic. You see it in the description of the blessed man in Psalm 1: "He is like a tree planted by streams of water that yields its fruit in its season. . . . In all that he does, he prospers" (v. 3). You also see productivity and fruit-bearing linked in the parable of the sower. In this story, Jesus speaks of the fruit of the seed which fell on good soil not just bearing fruit but doing so productively! It yields "in one case a hundredfold, in another sixty, and in another thirty" (Matt. 13:23). Productive fruit-bearing is the natural state for Christians.

My favorite passage for demonstrating the link between productivity and fruit-bearing is John 15. In verse 8, Jesus says this: "By this my Father is glorified, that you bear much fruit." This short verse brings together purpose, product, and productivity. We saw in chapter 3 that the purpose of our productivity is to glorify God, and that's just what Jesus has in mind here. Want to glorify God? Productively bear much fruit.

But what is the product or the content of our productivity? If you worked in one of Henry Ford's factories, the content of your productivity would be Model Ts; in your office job it might be reports, but in God's economy the content of our productivity is fruit. The crucial questions for the Christian who wants to be productive in glorifying God are these: What exactly is this fruit, and how do I bear more of it?

THE FRUIT OF GOOD WORKS

The context of John 15 is Jesus' famous declaration that He is the true vine. To understand the nature of the fruit discussed here, we need to grasp the four elements of this metaphor: the vine, the vinedresser, the branches, and the fruit.

The Vine & the Vinedresser

John 15:1 begins with Jesus saying, "I am the true vine, and my Father is the vinedresser." Here are elements one and two. Jesus is the vine and God the Father is the One who tends to the vineyard. The vinedresser is concerned about fruit. The purpose of a vineyard after all is not merely to grow a bunch of vines and branches. But grapes are a finicky fruit. You need the right climate and conditions to grow them. You also need to pay close attention to the plants themselves. The vinedresser's job was to ensure that the grape vines were as fruitful as possible. This involved making sure the branches were properly supported by the trellises as the grapes grew and became heavier, but it also meant pruning or removing parts of the plant that were not productive. Doing so allowed the nutrients from the vine to be focused on the parts that were bearing fruit. This is what the Father does; He plucks and prunes branches.

The Branches

Jesus continues the metaphor, saying, "Every branch in me that does not bear fruit he takes away, and every branch that does bear fruit he prunes, that it may bear more fruit" (John 15:2). The branches are disciples of Jesus Christ. The vinedresser removes the branches that do not bear fruit because their lack of fruit indicates that they are not truly connected to the vine. These branches refer to those who appear to be believers on the outside, meaning they've professed faith in Christ, but whose fruit proves that their faith is not genuine. Therefore, the vinedresser removes them from the vine.

As the metaphor implies, a true believer's union with Christ supplies the power to produce fruit. This speaks to the source of our productive power, something we will talk about more in chapter 7. Just as the branch draws its nourishment from the grapevine, so Christians are empowered to be productive by our connection to Christ. And the vinedresser does not pluck off the true branches but instead prunes them: "Every branch that does bear fruit he prunes, that it may bear more fruit." Through the providence of our experiences, trials, and the encouragement of other believers, the Father is at work to help believers be even more productive. What a joy to know that God not only calls me to be productive but supplies the power as well!

The Fruit

The fourth element of the true vine metaphor is the fruit, which is obedience. When we abide in Christ—meaning we are united to Him by faith, walking closely with Him, loving Him, and keeping His instructions close to our hearts—we bear the fruit of obedience (see John 15:7, 9–10). The fruit that pleases the Father, however, is not begrudging, servile obedience. He is pleased by full-hearted, willing obedience that manifests in our actions, attitudes, and even our thoughts. This fruit manifests in all three layers of the content of Christian productivity we talked about earlier—internal character, external obedience, and practical effectiveness. But there's a simpler way to refer to this fruit. This fruit is the same as what the Bible elsewhere calls "good works."

GOOD WORKS & THE GOSPEL

In the context of John 15, the fruit is clearly obedience to Jesus' commands (John 15:9–10, 12, 14). And when Jesus talks about how we glorify the Father elsewhere, He speaks of good works in the same way He speaks of bearing fruit: "In the same way, let your light shine before others, so that they may see your good works and give glory to your Father who is in heaven" (Matt. 5:16). Fruit equals good works. But the second we start talking about good works, Bible-believing Christians tend to start getting itchy. What do you mean good works? Aren't we saved by grace, not by works? Yes, we are saved by grace, but we are saved *unto* good works.

Ephesians 2:8–9 is one of most succinct statements of our salvation's basis in faith and not in our good works: "For by grace you have been saved through faith. And this is not your own doing; it is the gift of God, not a result of works, so that no one may boast." It is indeed God's free grace, appropriated through faith, that saves us from our sin. Paul goes out of his way to make it clear that salvation is "not a result of works, so that no one may boast." But that does not mean there is no place for good works in the Christian life. Quite the opposite! The apostle continues, "For we are his workmanship, created in Christ Jesus for good works, which God prepared beforehand, that we should walk in them" (v. 10). You were created to walk in good works. This is your purpose because good works are how we glorify God. They are the fruit you've been called to bear.

So, our good works do not contribute in any way to our salvation, but they do evidence that we are truly saved. Jesus indicated as much in John 15. When we bear fruit, we prove to be His disciples (John 15:8). James also emphasizes this point when he says, "faith by itself, if it does not have works, is dead" (James 2:17). James isn't saying you can lose your salvation or that good works somehow supplement your faith. He's arguing that faith is shown to be genuine by the good works it naturally bears. This is the organic view of personal productivity. It's not just that Christians *should* be productive; it's that Christians *are* productive. Because if we are connected to the true vine, we can't help but bear fruit. Productivity that pleases God is a natural outgrowth of your new nature in Jesus Christ.

Trees bear fruit according to their nature. "Can a fig tree, my brothers, bear olives, or a grapevine produce figs? Neither can a salt pond yield fresh water" (James 3:12). When we are saved, we are transformed into a new kind of tree. An unredeemed person only produces rotten fruit, but a Christian produces good fruit that is pleasing to God.[3] The Bible makes clear that being productive in good works is not a nice add-on but an integral part of what it means to be a Christian.

But what many Christians still miss is that demonstrating the genuineness of our faith is not the only purpose of good works. Good works are the stuff of the Christian life. It's what we are about, not just on Sunday but in every moment of every day. Believers in Jesus Christ who have an eternal perspective will do everything they can to become people who are productive in good works, because good works glorify God. This is part of God's purpose in saving us: "who gave himself for us to redeem us from all lawlessness and to purify for himself a people for his own possession who are zealous for good works" (Titus 2:14).

Good works certainly consist of the type of activities that might immediately jump to mind: serving others, sharing the gospel, teaching the Bible, etc. But the Scriptures make plain that good works are not reserved for the ultra-spiritual or full-time ministers. Good works are to make up the day-to-day lives of every true believer. Good works are the content of our productivity. As Matt Perman writes, "According to the Scriptures, good works are not simply the rare, special, extraordinary, or super-spiritual things we do. Rather, they are anything we do in faith."[4] And I agree with him when he says, "We can redefine productivity this way: to be productive is to be fruitful in good works."[5]

Good works are the mark of a productive Christian life. They are to adorn men and women who profess godliness (1 Tim. 2:10), the unmarried, the married, and the widow (1 Tim. 5:10), they are to be so common in us that they cannot be hidden (1 Tim. 5:25), and they are the mark of all who have dedicated themselves to God (2 Tim. 2:21; Titus 1:15–16). Good works show up in our everyday acts of generosity (Acts 9:36; 1 Tim. 6:18). But even though good works are the natural product of being connected to Christ by faith, they don't happen by accident. Christians are called "to devote themselves to good works" (Titus 3:8, 14) and instructed to be "ready for every good work" (Titus 3:1). We are to help one another be people of good works: "And let us consider how to stir one another to love and good works" (Heb. 10:24).

FOCUS ON THE ROOT NOT THE FRUIT

The power of the organic metaphor for productivity is that it throws pragmatism out the window. The branch produces fruit because it is rooted in the true vine. Believers are characterized by love and good works because of what the Holy Spirit is doing in us. You can't staple fruit to the branch of a grapevine and say, "Look what this vine produced!" First, this is the heart of hypocrisy. Insincere obedience is precisely what Jesus condemned in the Pharisees. Obedience disconnected from Christ is not obedience at all. Second, fake fruit is contemptuous because instead of bringing glory to God (the purpose of our productivity), it seeks to instead glorify the branch. It boasts, "Look at what a good and productive person I am." Understood properly, the content of God-honoring productivity must account for the root of productivity as well. And the root of all true and lasting productivity is Jesus Christ.

If we want to lead fruitful lives, we need to focus on the root not the fruit. If the vine is the source of our productivity, then maintaining the vitality of that connection is our prime directive. That's why the first practice we discussed had you begin your mornings with fellowship with God. Jesus said, "Apart from me you can do nothing" (John 15:5).

Yet even though it is God who enables us to be productive, we are still responsible for diligently walking with Him. Practical productivity tools like an alarm clock, calendar, or planner can help you walk with the Lord consistently. Think of tools and tactics as the trellises that support your fruitful branches. Productive Christians are firmly rooted in Christ, letting Him transform their character, and they make the most of the tools and opportunities presented to them that they might bear more of the fruit of good works for His glory.

As we seek to be faithful in our external obedience and practical effectiveness, taking hold of the tools of productivity is not a slight against the root. This is where the parable of the stewards and the talents helps balance the vine and branches metaphor. The power to be productive in our internal character comes from the true vine, but the responsibility for obedience and practical effectiveness is still ours. Once our understanding of the content of productivity has been redeemed, we are able to steward practical tools to assist us in our fruitful efforts instead of viewing practical effectiveness as the only content of our productivity.

Productive Christians redeem the content of productivity by considering it in organic terms, not mechanically. They recognize that the only productivity that will ultimately please God is that which comes from their union with Christ, the true vine. Our productivity starts with internal character, blossoms in external obedience, and overflows in practical effectiveness. What the world calls productivity in our work is merely a byproduct of something much deeper going on inside of us. This is the kind of fruit which pleases God, and He calls us to bear much of it.

6

TRACK YOUR COMMITMENTS

—— - - ——

When I was a kid, I had a recurring nightmare. Several times a week, I would have a dream in which a man would be chasing me, and when he caught me, I would be turned into chocolate. Some people may think there's deep psychological meaning to that dream. I sure hope not, because it was super weird. I'm glad I stopped having that dream, but another recurring dream that I still have to this day is some variation of what we'll call the "school-mare." I bet you've had some version of this dream before too. It's finals week and suddenly you realize there's a class that you had forgotten to attend all semester. You sweat through the exam, knowing you are completely unprepared and are most definitely going to flunk this class. Other versions of this dream include not being able to find your classroom, forgetting your locker combination, or committing the classic blunder of showing up to school without pants on.

While I've never heard of someone else having a dream about a man with a milk-chocolate Midas touch, I was relieved to find that school-mares are quite common—even in people who have been out of school for decades. In fact, the school-mare is among the five most common recurring dreams.[1] Sometimes called anxiety dreams, dreams like these stick with us even into adulthood because they express some of our deepest fears of embarrassment or failure. We are terrified of being unprepared.

We fear being unprepared because we know the sting of disappointment when we've let someone down. We've all had real-life experiences of dropping the ball. We've promised to do something and either forgotten about it or simply failed to follow through. No one wants the reputation of being undependable. And this urge is related to fruit-bearing.

In the last chapter, we talked about the fruit we've been called to bear for God and how it makes up the content of our productivity. Many of those good works, however, aren't just one-off acts. The fruit of a faithful Christian life shows up in the normal commitments we make to ourselves and others. We commit to do our jobs well, commit to serve in our churches, and commit to responsibilities in our homes. Being faithful in fruit-bearing, therefore, requires us to be faithful to our commitments. We want to be the kind of people who keep our commitments, but these days managing your commitments is harder than ever, for several reasons.

First, the world is increasingly complex. The sheer number of demands placed on us today is certainly unparalleled in human history. We can't possibly keep track of all the promises we've made in our heads while also fielding the bombardment of distractions vying for our already-divided attention. Yet that's exactly what we try to do. Someone at church asks you to do something. You say yes then promptly forget all about it. Your boss asks if you have the bandwidth to take on another project. You say yes, then a week later you find yourself sheepishly waiting outside his door to explain why you got too busy to finish his project on time.

Second, our brains weren't designed to hold so many commitments at once. David Allen's Getting Things Done methodology uses the tagline, "Your mind is for having ideas, not holding them."[2] I think he's right. God designed our brains to be incredible processing organs. We can come up with amazing ideas and solve complex problems, but memory is another story. The capacity of our short-term memory is remarkably limited. How often have you gone into another room intent on doing something only to stand in the doorway with no idea why you went there? For me, there seems to be something about walking up a staircase that wipes my brain clean.

Third, our inability to keep track of our commitments is compounded by the noetic effects of sin, which is a fancy way of saying sin makes us stupid. In Genesis 3, we read how God cursed the work of our hands (vv. 17–19), but those thistles and thorns did not only affect agricultural work. The curse affected our brains too. This is what theologians call the noetic effects of the fall. Noetic comes from the Greek word *gnosis*, meaning knowledge. Because of sin, me no think good no more. If that previous sentence isn't evidence enough, compare how easy it is to forget someone's name seconds after you've met them to how Adam (before the curse) named and remembered *every single animal* in existence (Gen. 2:20)! Because of sin, mankind has a memory problem.

If we are going to bear much fruit in this complex world with these broken brains, we need a method for getting those commitments out of our heads and into a system that won't let us forget them. That's what this chapter is all about: the practice of building a task management system. I'll show you a simple system that will help you get more done, become more dependable, and feel less stressed.

OPEN LOOPS & BROKEN PROMISES

There's a funny thing you'll notice if you start watching for it—the days you feel the most productive aren't the days you did the greatest number of things but the days you got the most things done. Read that sentence again slowly. There is a world of difference between doing a lot of things and getting a lot of things done. Productivity isn't about running from task to task like a chicken with its head cut off; productivity is about completion. We're talking about getting things done, not getting things started. And the more things you have unfinished at any given time, the more stressed you will feel.

When things are left incomplete, we struggle to forget about them. It's why you have to finish the song when someone starts humming a tune. It's the reason fiction writing contains multiple plotlines. Every time one plotline is ending, a new one is just beginning, and you have to keep reading because you crave resolution. And it's the reason why when you have an undone task, you can't stop thinking about it. We need things to be complete so we can forget about them. This phenomenon is what psychologists call the Zeigarnik effect. It's the brain's tendency to remember incomplete tasks but forget them once they are complete.

The modern world is an ocean of incomplete tasks, and our brains weren't made to swim in such deep waters.

Our brains don't care how important or unimportant a task is, just that it's incomplete. So, the more undone things you have on your plate the more distracted you will feel, even if they aren't that important.[3]

There are good aspects of the Zeigarnik effect, like when we wake up in the middle of the night wondering, "Did I lock the door?" But our craving for completion presents problems when we have too many incomplete tasks. Our brains can't manage more than a handful of incomplete tasks at any given time. This poses a major problem in our always-connected information age. You have a whirlwind of stuff coming at you all the time—emails, requests, calls to return, commitments to fulfill, and much more. Add to that all the other open loops that entertainment and social media feeds create in our minds, and it's a wonder we can get anything done.

The modern world is an ocean of incomplete tasks, and our brains weren't made to swim in such deep waters.

The first step to overcoming this problem is to understand why it's happening. It's one thing to call it a fancy name like the Zeigarnik effect, but *why* is it we can't forget incomplete tasks? In short, we crave completion because we long to keep our promises. We want our "yes" to be "yes" (Matt. 5:37). Every item on your list, whether assigned to you by someone else or created by yourself, is a little promise. We were made in the image of a promise-keeping God. Our brains are designed to remind us about our commitments and promises until they are fulfilled. And remind us they do, even when we are trying to focus on something else. But because modern life requires us to remember too many commitments at once, we get overwhelmed and commitments get broken.

Thankfully, there is a solution! Join your local monastery.

Just kidding.

There's another solution that doesn't require you to leave modern society behind or wear an itchy robe. You need to store unfinished obligations outside of your brain in a trusted system. A quirk in the human brain allows us to let go of tasks if we are confident they won't be forgotten. This is how you can leverage the Zeigarnik effect to your advantage. Sönke Ahrens explains,

Thanks to Zeigarnik's follow-up research, we also know that we don't actually have to finish tasks to convince our brains to stop thinking about them. All we have to do is to write them down in a way that convinces us that it will be taken care of. That's right: The brain doesn't distinguish between an actual finished task and one that is postponed by taking a note. By writing something down, we literally get it out of our heads.[4]

Essentially, you can trick your brain into treating a task as complete if you get it out of your short-term memory. A trusted task management system, therefore, is one of the most important productivity tools you can have in your arsenal, enabling you to think more clearly, execute more effectively, and ultimately become much better at keeping your word. It allows your brain to chill and you to get back to work. Having a clear set of rules in place for managing your commitments can help you become a more dependable parent, a more thoughtful pastor, a more faithful worker, or simply someone who consistently does what you say you will do. Let me show you how to set one up.[5]

FEATURES OF A GOOD TASK MANAGEMENT SYSTEM

Many people think just downloading a reminders app on their phone is enough to track their commitments. But the power of any productivity system is not in the tools you use but in how you use the tools. So, let's begin with the principles that make for a good task management system. These principles can be applied whether you're using the latest task management app or a regular old pen and paper.[6]

There are five features every good task management system should have. And they follow the convenient acronym REDEEM.[7] Because what kind of productivity guru would I be if I didn't give you acronyms?

Reliable

For your mind to focus, you need to have confidence that your commitments really won't be forgotten forever, lost, or destroyed. So, whether you use software or pen and paper, protect that store of ideas diligently. It must be reliable.

External

Get your commitments out of your head. I've heard of some people who try to keep their commitments in their brain by using mnemonic devices or memory palaces. That may be more effective than leaving it to chance, but there's no reason to do that. Just get it completely out of your brain. Remember, your brain is for having ideas not for storing them.

Doable

The way you write your tasks in your system should be clear and actionable. Begin with a verb. "*Call* the repairman." "*Write* the first draft." "*Code* the home page." These tasks should require minimal interpretation so that when you look at them days, weeks, or months in the future, you know exactly what to do next. This reinforces the reliability of the system and assists your brain in letting go.

Exhaustive

There should be only one place where you capture and review your tasks. If you have some tasks in this app, some on that note pad, and some on sticky notes, your trust in the system will break down and you will default to trying to keep all the tasks in your head again. Use only one place to corral tasks.

Engaging

A good task management system should invite you to do focused work, not overwhelm or confuse you. If your system becomes overly complicated or filled with overdue tasks you never really plan on getting to, you will stop using it. Aesthetics are important here too. If you find joy in writing with a pen and paper, then get a fancy notebook and pen and have at it. If you like a clean minimal app, then invest in that. Make it so you *want* to use your task management system.

Manageable

Your task management system should be simple enough to provide clarity amid chaos. When all your plans for the day fall apart, your task management system should be the place you go to reorient yourself to the next thing that needs doing. If your system itself is in a state of chaos, it will add to the mayhem instead of providing relief from it.

Now, let me show you a framework that meets these criteria and has worked well for me and for many others to whom I've taught it.

YOUR FIVE LISTS

Whether you're using an advanced task tracking app or just a piece of paper, every good task management system should have clearly defined steps. If you want to keep your tasks organized, you need a framework that aligns with those REDEEM principles. The task management framework below follows the acronym COPE:

1. **C**entralize
2. **O**rganize
3. **P**rioritize
4. **E**xecute

The COPE framework above utilizes five lists: an inbox, a projects list, an actions list, a future list, and a daily list. If you follow the four steps using these five lists, you won't drop the ball on commitments nearly as often, and you'll enjoy a focus and clarity around your work that is tremendously freeing! Let's briefly look at the purpose of each list, then I'll show you how they work within each step of the COPE framework.

Chances are you utilize some type of to-do list. There are many benefits to having a to-do list, but having just one isn't enough. A fully functioning task management system requires five types of lists. You can do these with paper and pen, but most task management apps either allow for these lists or build them into the app in some way. Still, most users of task management apps don't utilize all five lists properly because they don't have a framework for when to use which list.

Inbox

The first list is where you initially capture tasks. It's a repository where you store any fleeting idea, would-be task, or request. For me, the Things app on my phone serves this purpose, but for a long time I just used a simple notebook that I carried in my back pocket. It doesn't matter what you use for your inbox list as long as it meets the REDEEM criteria and you are using it to capture tasks as soon as they come up. Your inbox list is fleeting; everything on this list will be processed later.

Projects List

When you begin organizing your tasks, you'll need to group them together. Often, what you initially thought was a task should really be a project, a grouping of multiple tasks. Keeping a list of all your current projects is crucial to avoid overcommitment. Again, you can keep this list on a piece of paper, or just about any to-do list software has an area that shows all active projects with their list of tasks embedded beneath them like a folder.

Actions List

The actions list comprises the individual steps you need to *do* to bring a project to completion. As David Allen says, "Many projects seem overwhelming—and are overwhelming—because you can't do a project at all! You can only do an action related to it."[8] Each of your projects will have an actions list. To keep these specific and actionable, write them as sentences beginning with a verb. For example, if one of your projects is "Plan Trip to Rome," your actions might be:

1. *Add* trip dates to calendar
2. *Request* time off from boss
3. *Read* travel guides
4. *Create* daily itinerary
5. *Book* hotel room

We'll talk more about how to organize and clarify these actions in the organize step of the COPE framework.

Future List

You can't do everything at once, but just because you can't currently act on a project doesn't mean you should try to keep it in your head. Some inbox items, projects, or actions should be migrated to a future list. These are things you can't do right now but want to remove from your brain to somewhere you will check again. I'll show you how you can make sure your future list doesn't become a graveyard for good intentions in a moment, but we have one more list to cover first. And it's the most important one of all.

Daily List

Plans are great, but until you start doing them, they remain merely wishes. The daily list is where the action is at. If you're using a to-do list app, this might be called your "today" list. As the name suggests, these are the actions and projects you plan to work on today. This list should be short and clear. Personally, I like to manually copy my daily list from my to-do list software into my paper notebook. That way I don't get distracted by all the other things I *could* be doing on my projects list. The purpose of the daily list is to force you to prioritize, to decide at the beginning of the day, "This is what I'm working on."

THE COPE FRAMEWORK IN PRACTICE

Okay, I know that was a lot of theory. But stick with me, because now we'll see how it works in practice. I promise that if you can grasp these concepts, you will become a true to-do list ninja. Now let's see how to put these lists into action using the four steps of the COPE framework.

Step 1: Centralize

The first step in any task management system is to capture and centralize every new potential commitment that enters your life. This step utilizes your inbox. This list needs to be external and exhaustive. When a task pops into your head or you agree to a new commitment, even if you may decide not to do it later, write it down! But not just anywhere. It's essential to centralize all of your to-dos in *one* place because tasks arrive in a myriad of forms. Here are a few common places you might find tasks buried:

- Emails
- Calls
- In-person conversations

- Memos
- Texts
- Meeting notes
- Stray shower thoughts
- Upcoming calendar events

The goal of the centralize step is to train yourself such that when you think, "Oh, I need to do something about that," you immediately make a note about it in your inbox. When you do this consistently, you will find your brain feeling much clearer. But to maintain that sense of calm and actually get done what you write on that list, you need to do the next step.

Step 2: Organize

In chapter 4, we talked about the importance of being organized. Organization is just as important when it comes to your commitments as it is for your environment. If you don't know what you've already agreed to do, you'll either take on too much and become overcommitted or refuse new commitments because you feel busier than you actually are. Organizing your commitments is a stewardship issue. You may have captured everything in a centralized inbox, but if that list turns into a giant mess of unrelated tasks, you'll quickly become overwhelmed. That's why organization is step two in the COPE framework.

An organized to-do list allows you to do two things: first, quickly identify the status of a commitment, and second, view your tasks in logical groups. To organize your inbox, ask yourself five questions about each commitment.

Am I still committed to this? If no, delete it. If yes, move on to question two.

What is my definition of done? Rewrite the task with as much clarity as possible, describing what it would look like if it was done. Instead of "Get back to Mark," write something like "Call Mark and ask him about the date for the picnic."

Will this take more than one action to complete? If yes, your task is actually a project and should be moved to your projects list. If no, it remains in your general actions list.

What's the next action? Whether it's a project or a task, think carefully and specifically about what the next physical action should be. Often, we fail to act because we've actually written down the second or third step. Maybe you wrote "Pay the bills" when the next action is actually "Gather all the bills together in one place." Lack of clarity leads to lack of action. Taking ten seconds to define the next physical action is often all that's needed to get a long-neglected project moving again.

Can I do this right now? If so, then do it. If not, file it with your projects or in a future list.

Okay, now we're getting organized! But we still need to decide the order in which we'll get all these tasks and projects done. That brings us to step three, prioritize.

Step 3: Prioritize

One way we procrastinate our commitments is by having more than one priority. One often overlooked benefit of keeping lists of your commitments is that lists inherently force you to prioritize. There can only be one item at the top of a list. In step three of COPE, you will arrange your organized projects and actions by priority.

Our priorities are constantly shifting as new commitments come onto our radar, so the act of prioritizing is an ongoing dance. But there are three primary times when you should do this step. First, prioritization should happen at the beginning of the day when you

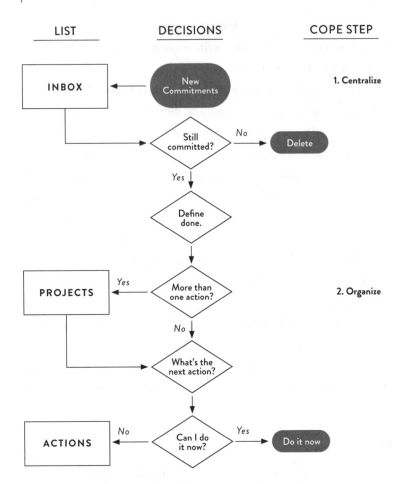

Figure 6.1: COPE Centralize & Organize Flowchart

choose what's most important on your list and move it to your daily list. Second, you will prioritize throughout your day. As you complete the next most important thing on your daily list, you will reevaluate what gets promoted to the new most important thing. Third, you will prioritize during your weekly review, which we'll cover in a moment.

The prioritization phase consists of two steps: First, move projects

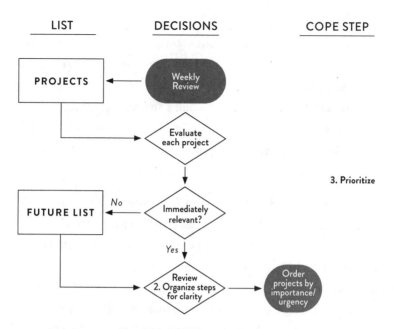

Figure 6.2: COPE Prioritize Flow Chart

that are not immediately relevant to your future list (don't worry, the future list will be evaluated weekly). Second, order the remaining items on your projects list according to importance (gauge importance in terms of your long-term goals).

Step 4: Execute

After you follow the first three steps, you'll have a list of tasks that are all in one place, organized into projects, and prioritized by importance. This will allow you to do the final and most important step of all—execute. A to-do list that doesn't enable you to actually *do* is useless. This is the step where we utilize the **Daily List**.

Here are the five steps that make up the execute phase. You'll do these at the beginning and end of each day.

1. Survey your **Projects List**.
2. Copy the next actions for one to three projects to the **Daily List**.
3. Decide which *one* action is most important and make time to do that first.
4. Return to your list of next actions and repeat step three.
5. Take five minutes at the end of the day to go back through your projects list and redefine the next actions for any projects you've worked on today.

Personally, even though I use an app to keep track of all my projects and actions, I like to copy my daily list in a paper notebook, because when I'm in execute mode, I don't want to be distracted by all the things I could be doing. Throughout the day, I put a star next to the most important task. Once that's finished, I put a star by the next important task. At the end of the day, I look back at my projects list and make sure the next action is clear for any projects I worked on that day. Tomorrow, I'll do the exact same thing. This keeps me organized and helps me make progress on what's most important every day instead of just drifting from one urgent distraction to the next. But no matter how well I try to keep up with this system each day, it still needs weekly maintenance.

WEEKLY REVIEWS

The linchpin of any to-do list management system is regular reviews. Without a regular review, you will lose trust in your system and it will cease to serve you. Even though you'll be looking at your projects and actions daily as you choose what to work on, it's still wise to schedule a weekly review to keep your task management system shipshape. This ensures that nothing is forgotten and that you always know what needs to be done next.

I recommend scheduling a weekly review on your calendar at the end of each week. For me, a weekly review is the last thing I do on Fridays. As I mentioned in chapter 4, Friday afternoon is also the time when I tidy up my workspace. Reviewing things at the end of the work week lets me come out of a work mindset for the weekend while still leaving myself a trail of breadcrumbs for next week, so I know exactly where I left off when I return on Monday.

Utilize the following steps in your weekly review sessions.

1. Deal with Loose Ends

Centralize everything into your inbox. Process your paper inbox if you have one. Review any meeting notes, loose papers, or stray thoughts you've jotted down, capturing specific tasks into your inbox. Review your email inbox. Try to get to inbox zero, or create actions for emails you aren't sure about. Actionable items should be on your inbox list, events should go on your calendar, and important information you may need to reference later should be stored in an appropriate place. The goal here is to get everything off your mind and into the proper system so next week begins with a blank slate.

2. Look Ahead

Next, look at your calendar for the next two to three weeks. What's coming up? Are there any events that require some prep work ahead of time? If so, create tasks and projects for those so they don't sneak up on you. Look at your projects list. Do any of your projects have due dates that are becoming urgent? What deadlines are approaching? What projects can you drop? What projects are stalled out and may need follow-up next week? Make actions for each of these.

3. Reflect on the Week

If you're always looking forward, you'll never take the time to praise the Lord for the wins or adjust after the losses. As part of my weekly review, I like to spend time reflecting on the week that's ending. I do this in my journal by taking a few minutes to write the highs and lows of the week. What habits are working? Which ones aren't? Where could I improve things? How has my walk with the Lord been? How are my relationships going? This is a chance to be honest with yourself. It's a checkup not just on your work but also on your soul. Many people go years without evaluating how things are going. Imagine what would happen if you didn't let a single week go by without pausing to reflect.

4. Get Creative

At this point in your weekly review, something magical will start to happen. You'll feel your shoulders loosening. You've reframed your worries into actionable plans that you know you'll pick up on next week. At this point I start to feel a little giddy, because once my head is clear, I experience a flood of creative ideas. Often our creativity is blocked because we're using all of our brain's resources trying to hold all of our commitments in our head. When we organize those commitments into their proper place and are confident we will get to them at the appropriate time, our creativity is unshackled. Have you ever noticed that some of your best ideas form when you're on vacation? It's because your mind is free from the daily grind. Completing my weekly review on Friday afternoon puts my mind into mini-vacation mode. Don't let this time go to waste! Capture those ideas in your inbox. Leave a trail for yourself so you can pick up on those ideas after the weekend.

5. *Pray*

Finally, spend some time thanking the Lord for the previous week. Thank Him for the opportunity to serve others, to glorify Him, and to enjoy the gift of meaningful work. Ask Him for help to improve where you've fallen short, and seek wisdom from Him for the next week. Now go enjoy a restful weekend to the glory of God!

Following the COPE framework ensures that your daily schedule is not dominated by the tyranny of the urgent. Instead, you are forcing yourself to make a little progress on your most important projects each day. Remember, to-do lists were made for man, not man for to-do lists. Your commitment management system is a helpful tool, but it's just a tool. Even if you always use it right, you still won't be able to get everything done. And that's okay.

No matter how good we get at keeping up with our commitments, we'll always fall short. But God loves us based on how perfect His Son and His sacrifice were, not on how perfectly productive we were today. I can stand before God and men with confidence, even in my daily failure to live up to my own standards, because Christ has lived up to God's standards on my behalf. Nevertheless, as a faithful steward, I'll keep struggling to make the most of each day in His power and for His glory. And I'll use whatever tools I can find to help me do that better.

PILLAR 4

THE SOURCE OF PRODUCTIVITY

You Are Uniquely Gifted by God

——— – – ———

Productivity-minded people tend to focus on what they don't have. It's a natural byproduct of ambition. You want to get more, find more success, and refine yourself, so you're always reaching for the next thing. Because of this, we focus primarily on improving our weaknesses. And while it's good to want to get better where we fall short, the downside of this mindset is that it can cause us to underestimate the unique way God has gifted us. Instead of flourishing in our strengths, we spend our time wishing we had so-and-so's gifts instead.

In their 2020 book, *The Unfair Advantage,* authors Hasan Hubba and Ash Ali suggest to entrepreneurs an alternative approach to competition. Instead of trying to compete against the strengths of other businesses, they encourage their readers to focus their attention on their own unique strengths. By leaning into your unfair advantages, you can develop a unique identity that's difficult to copy. I believe God has provided Christians with unique productivity advantages.

Sometimes we fail to see just how much productive power God has given us because we are too focused on the latest and best productivity systems the world offers. If we are going to redeem productivity from the world, we need to talk about the believer's unique sources of productive power.

The world says be productive in your own strength, but the Bible says be productive in God's power. We saw this in the metaphor of the vine and branches in John 15. Christians cannot produce fruit by their own efforts; it's only via their connection to Christ that they can do anything that truly matters (John 15:5). Believers in Jesus Christ know that "it is God who works in you, both to will and to work for his good pleasure" (Phil. 2:13). God-honoring productivity is fueled by His power working through me for His glory.

There may be a lot to be gained from the world's methods, but every believer already holds several unfair advantages when it comes to personal productivity.

The power to produce the fruit of good works in our jobs, homes, churches, and neighborhoods isn't found in this technique or that system; it's found in the sufficient grace granted to us in Christ Jesus. "And God is able to make all grace abound to you, so that having all sufficiency in all things at all times, you may abound in every good work" (2 Cor. 9:8). Christians already have what it takes to be productive. God has equipped us to "abound in every good work." So, for the Christian, productivity is not primarily about being the strongest, smartest, or hardest working. It's about drawing on God's power to serve others and bring Him glory.

One thing I've come to appreciate as I've studied what the Bible has to say about productivity is that God has specially equipped believers for the task.

There may be a lot to be gained from the world's methods, but every believer already holds several unfair advantages when it comes to personal productivity.

Some of these advantages are common to all Christians, and some are unique to each individual. Let's first look at some of the unfair productivity advantages every Christian possesses.

AMAZING GRACE

The first unfair productivity advantage Christians have is that we are under grace. Those who have placed their faith in Jesus Christ have a new relationship to their work. Many people employ productivity techniques out of fear—fear of failure, fear of financial ruin, or fear of embarrassment. But because Christ has paid the penalty for our sins, we've got nothing to fear. Perfect love has cast it out (1 John 4:18). Christians know that our identity is not in our ability to get stuff done but in Christ's "It is finished" (John 19:30). What a relief!

Still, we often look to productivity to find peace. We think that if we work hard enough, we can find the peace of financial security, respect from the world, or just some relief from life's daily pressures. But by grace, we already have peace through Jesus Christ. Our productivity, therefore, becomes an expression of quiet worship, not desperation. When we have a bad day, don't finish our to-do list, or miss a goal, we don't beat ourselves up about it—we turn it over to God. Christ is the basis of our peace, not our productivity.

POWERFUL PRAYER

The second unfair productivity advantage Christians have is prayer. The veil is torn; we now have access to God the Father through Jesus Christ. "Let us then with confidence draw near to the throne of grace, that we may receive mercy and find grace to help in time of need" (Heb. 4:16). And prayer isn't just another weapon in our productivity arsenal, it's a tactical nuke. Yet too few of us take advantage of it. Not only is being able to talk to God an unimaginable privilege, but prayer is also supernaturally effective. James 5:16 says, "The prayer of a righteous person is powerful and effective" (NIV). Prayer works. If our aim is to be productive in bearing good fruit for God's glory, why wouldn't we take advantage of the resources He gave us to accomplish that mission? Too often we set out in pursuit of our goals or daily plan without pausing to seek heavenly aid. If God wants you to be productive and He promises to provide assistance if you ask, then why don't we pray more?

Imagine if we prayed throughout the day at work. Imagine if we were disciplined in asking the Lord to establish the work of our hands (Ps. 90:17). What would happen if we wrote time to pray into our daily schedules and took it just as seriously as we take our lunch breaks or Zoom meetings? Of the many things you can squeeze onto your to-do list, does prayer make the cut? Prayer is indeed an unfair productivity advantage. If only we took prayer more seriously.

CLEAR PURPOSE

We talked about this at length in chapter 3, but knowing why you are here on this planet is an unbelievable advantage. While the rest of the world gropes for meaning or seeks to construct its own sense of purpose, we have ours etched in stone. We know exactly why we are here. We exist to glorify God. Having that north star of purpose can save the productive Christian from countless griefs. When our ultimate aim is the fame of the Maker, we will steer clear of traps like the love of money, vainglory, or corner cutting. Productive Christians get up and work each day because we know that ultimately our work brings glory to the King we so love. Knowing our purpose gives Christians an unfair productivity advantage.

GUARANTEED SUCCESS

Finally, every Christian has the unfair productivity advantage of knowing our success is guaranteed. Believers are on a can't-fail mission. As we seek to manage our time well and be efficient and productive, we are constantly committing our work to God and trusting that He will establish our plans (Prov. 16:3). But following the Lord does not mean you will always succeed in the short term. Your business may fail, you might fail the assignment, or your boss may hate your presentation. Following Jesus does not guarantee temporal success, but it does guarantee eternal success. "For everyone who has been born of God overcomes the world. And this is the victory that has overcome the world—our faith" (1 John 5:4).

The ending has already been written, and the winner is Jesus Christ and His followers. When we work in a manner worthy of our calling with right motives, even if our immediate plans fail, we have succeeded where it matters most. Productive Christians have an eternal perspective on success. Because of this we have the amazing ability to dust ourselves off with a joyful heart even after an epic failure.

SPIRITUAL GIFTS

Grace, prayer, purpose, and an eternal perspective on success are unfair productivity advantages that every believer has in common. But you have even more unfair advantages that are unique to you. Namely, your spiritual gifts. Every individual believer has been uniquely gifted by God to be productive in a particular way. We all have certain natural giftings.

You may be naturally intelligent, have a knack for basketball, or be good with numbers, and these giftings should be stewarded. But spiritual gifts are different. Coupled with your natural giftings, spiritual gifts should have tremendous bearing on where you focus your productive efforts.

There are at least seven lists of spiritual gifts in the New Testament, and no two are exactly the same. This has led theologians to conclude that these lists are not exhaustive but representative of a broad range of gifts.[1] Some of these lists speak of giftings for certain offices in the church, such as apostles, prophets, and teachers (Eph. 4:11). Other lists speak more generally of spiritual gifts distributed to every believer. Romans 12:6–8, for example, deals with gifts like exhorting, giving, leading, and mercy. In 1 Peter 4:10–11, gifts include speaking and serving, and 1 Corinthians 12 talks about gifts of wisdom, knowledge, faith, discernment, and helping.

Some of these lists also include what we might call "sign gifts." These are things like tongues, miracles, prophecy, and the gift of healing. These gifts were unique to the early church, as their miraculous nature served to authenticate the new revelation being given through the apostles during the writing of the New Testament. But don't let that confuse you. Those gifts may have put on a bigger show, but *all* spiritual gifts are of supernatural origin.

Spiritual gifts aren't just talents or characteristics like "I'm good with numbers" or "God made me tall." The Holy Spirit indwells believers and empowers them with specific spiritual gifts *as He chooses.* "All these are empowered by one and the same Spirit, who apportions to each one individually as he wills" (1 Cor. 12:11). What's amazing about this verse is that it means your spiritual gifting was handpicked by God the Holy Spirit *for you specifically*! Just like a drag racing car is fitted with special tires and other parts to equip it to be the fastest it can be on a short track, you've been supernaturally prepared for a specific calling. God has given you a grand purpose in making you to glorify Him, and He has specially equipped you to carry out that mission in a distinctive way. Therefore, your gift or combination of gifts is a stewardship unique to you. Just as the car built for drag racing would lose terribly in a 500-mile IndyCar race, when we don't play to the strengths of our spiritual gifts, we are hurting our productive potential.

Now, I want to be quick to note here that the primary purpose of our spiritual gifts is the good of other believers. "As each has received a gift, use it to serve one another, as good stewards of God's varied grace" (1 Peter 4:10). These gifts aren't to be used for our self-aggrandizement but instead for the good of others, particularly the body of believers (1 Cor. 12:7). Nevertheless, I believe our gifts have utility outside of the church walls as well.

Our spiritual gifts serve a secondary purpose by helping us to determine the focus of our productive efforts in all of life. You will find the most fulfillment and opportunity for productive, God-honoring labor if you take all your giftings into account, including your spiritual gifts. If the content of our productivity is to be good works, and good works are largely concerned with serving others, and spiritual gifts are the unique way you've been gifted to serve others, then we'd be crazy not to use them. Your spiritual gifts are your unfair productivity advantage. Here are a few ways to make full use of your spiritual gifts to productively glorify God.

Know Your Gifts

To use your gifts, you first must know what they are. Unfortunately, an angel doesn't show up when you get saved and hand you a little scroll that says, "Your spiritual gift is _____." Discovering your giftings is a process. First, as you look at the lists of spiritual gifts in the Scriptures, do any of them jump out to you as something you are particularly good at or find joy in? Start by experimenting with those gifts.

Second, are there certain gifts your Christian friends or pastors frequently identify in you? I would never have had any idea I was gifted to teach if my youth pastor hadn't basically forced me to lead a short devotional one week (thanks, Mark). Since spiritual gifts are primarily used within the body of Christ, other members of the body are best equipped to help us identify where we uniquely fit in.

Third, pray about your gifts. If you genuinely desire to serve Him by stewarding your gifts well, God will help you understand where you can best be used by Him.

Fourth, try serving in different ways. You might think you are gifted in leadership, but no one ever listens to you, or you might think you're gifted in mercy, but you are the last one to notice when someone is suffering. You won't know unless you try. Even if certain areas of service don't interest you initially, give yourself a chance to put your gifts to the test.

Use Your Gifts Like a Filter

Once you know where you are particularly gifted, there are several ways you can use that knowledge to decide where to dedicate your productive efforts. If we really wanted to start with our unfair advantage, we'd begin by identifying how we can utilize our spiritual gifts to maximize our fruit of good works.

In this world of endless options, we can quickly become paralyzed. What job should I do? Where should I live? Should I work on this or that? The myriad choices of our age are both a blessing and a curse. What good are endless options if they make it impossible for us to ever choose a course? We need filters, and our strengths are a great place to start.

If you're good with cars, perhaps you should be a mechanic. If you're good with numbers, maybe something in accounting would suit you. In the same way, knowing your spiritual gifts can give you clues as to where you might choose to dedicate yourself. If your spiritual gift is administration, then first serve the church with that, but also consider how you might bring that into your work and home as well. Or if you're gifted in hospitality, again, first serve the church with that. But it might also mean you can find meaningful work and ministry in the world by serving others and making them feel at home.

> *The world says that we can be productive in our own power, but Christians recognize that God is the power source of our productivity.*

Seek Opportunities That Best Utilize Your Gifts

Finally, you should proactively seek opportunities to use your gifts. If you have a gifting, don't wait for someone to come ask. Humbly let your church know how you believe you are gifted and make yourself available to be used in that way. Likewise, look for ways to use your gifts in your neighborhood, workplace, and home. If you're gifted to lead, then seek out leadership opportunities at work. If you're gifted in exhortation, find a way to be an encouragement to your neighbors. If you're gifted in wisdom, seek opportunities to pass that on to your children. The key word here is proactive. Sometimes we can feel presumptuous in offering our gifts, like we are bragging or stepping out of line, but offering to use your gifts is part of stewarding them well.

The world says that we can be productive in our own power, but Christians recognize that God is the power source of our productivity.

If you want to redeem productivity, you need to leverage your unfair advantages. Making use of all that God has given you is not just a good idea, it's the way you were designed to glorify God. He doesn't want us trying to serve Him in our own power.

When we are productive in God's power, putting our spiritual gifts to full use, God is doubly glorified. First, He is glorified in that we are seeking to serve Him. Second, He is glorified in that we cannot brag that our accomplishments came by our own effort. When people ask, "How are you able to get so much done?" the productive Christian's first answer isn't to name this system or that technique but to simply say, "It is God who is at work in me both to will and to work according to His good pleasure" (see Phil. 2:13). He is the source of our productive power.

PRACTICE 4

SET YOUR GOALS

—— - - ——

We all have goals, whether or not they are extremely ambitious or well-defined and regardless of if we say them aloud or write them down. A goal is simply a desire to go from one place or state of being to another. If you're taking a road trip, your goal is to go from here to there. If it's nearing lunchtime for you, your goal might be as simple as going from hungry to full. These are short-term goals, but we all have long-term goals as well. We have goals for our careers, health, finances, spiritual conditions, and much more. But too often our goals lack definition. And goals that lack clarity are goals that don't get done.

There is a science to setting good goals, but few of us have ever taken the time to consider how to create effective goals or set up systems that will allow us to achieve the results we want from them. More importantly, too few of us have considered how we should think about our goals as Christians.

In this chapter, we will look at the fourth practice of productive Christians—setting God-honoring goals. We will look at the biblical mindset for goal setting and dispel some common myths about goals. Then, I'll show you a step-by-step plan for creating goals you'll actually stick with. But first, we need to answer a question: Should we even be setting goals?

ARE GOALS POINTLESS?

There are many people who are flagrantly anti-goal, and to be fair, they have some pretty good arguments for why they believe the practice of goal setting is bunk. Here are a few of the most common arguments against setting goals:

- By setting goals, you're trying to control what you can't control.
- Goals can be disconnected from your larger purpose in life.
- Having goals will just stress you out.
- Chasing goals makes you unhappy.

If you've ever set a goal and failed to reach it, maybe you resonate with some of those statements. Anyone who has made a New Year's resolution only to break it two weeks later couldn't be blamed for thinking goals are pointless. However, none of the objections above disprove the effectiveness of goals. They have more to do with the way we go about setting goals. In fact, just about every argument I've ever heard against setting goals takes issue with the *how* and not the *what* of goal setting.

When used correctly, goal setting is one of the most effective productivity tools there is. But even if we learn all the best techniques for setting and reaching our goals, we still face a real temptation to idolize them. Goals can become a problem when we put our faith in them instead of in God.

GOAL SETTING & THE GLORY OF GOD

If we want to get goals right, we need to remember why we are here in the first place. This goes back to our second pillar of Christian productivity: you exist to glorify God. Our ultimate goal and the entire purpose for being productive is the glory of God. This means that every goal we make should be subordinate to that chief end. In addition, our definition of success in our goals will need to be redefined. Productive Christians judge the success of their goals based on whether they contributed to bringing God glory.

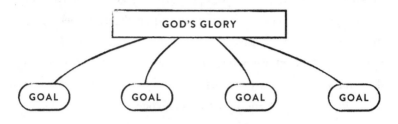

Figure 8.1: From Goals to Glory

If you imagine the Christian life like the voyage of a ship, then God's glory is the destination. Whatever else may happen along the way, that objective doesn't change. You may alter your course and encounter dramatic setbacks, but the only criterion for success is whether you reach that destination. God's glory determines the aim of your productive efforts. There are many paths you can take to get there, but each leg of your journey should be directed toward the goal of goals, God's glory. The ultimate purpose of your life, as we saw in chapter 3, is to make God look good. And your goals are an opportunity to show that God is a God worthy of your service.

If God's glory is your destination, then your goals are the waypoints. They help you chart a course toward God's glory. In the old days, a ship captain with a long voyage ahead of him wouldn't just plop an "X" on the map and say, "That's our destination. Let's aim the boat and start sailing!" Instead, he would strategically chart a course. First, he'd plan to stop at this port to resupply. Next, he'd plan to go around that cape and stop at that port to wait out the winter. Finally, he would complete the last leg to reach the destination. Each of these stops is a waypoint, a point along the journey that represents a step toward the overall goal. The problem with the way most Christians set goals is that we do it completely irrespective of our ultimate purpose.

If God's glory is your destination and your goals are the waypoints, the third important factor is your propulsion. Your productive habits and the systems you use are like your sail and oars, propelling you toward your goals. It would be futile for a captain to merely chart a course to the next waypoint if he had no means of propulsion. In the same way, your goals will be fruitless if you write them down but never actually implement the systems and habits that will enable you to make progress on them each day.

HOW TO SET GOOD GOALS

Now, let me show you how to apply these principles and set God-honoring goals that you'll actually stick with.

1. Write & Evaluate

The first thing you need to do is write your goal down. This is no minor step. Researchers have found that individuals who write their goals down are 42.1 percent more likely to reach them than those who don't.[1] Writing your goals down works because it forces you to clarify them. Too often what we call goals are really just vague wishes, like "I want to lose weight." That's not a goal. You need to ask some questions to force yourself to make it crystal clear.

A popular framework for clarifying written goals is to follow the acronym SMART.[2] Look at your goal and rewrite it in a way that meets each of these qualities:

- **S**pecific: Make it clear
- **M**easurable: Make it quantifiable

- **A**chievable: Make it realistic
- **R**elevant: Make it matter
- **T**ime-Bound: Make it stop

Asking the following questions, which correspond with each letter of the acronym, can help make sure your goal addresses all of those criteria.

- What state do I want to achieve with this goal?
- How will I quantify my progress?
- What resources do I need to reach this goal?
- How does this goal contribute to my calling and God's glory?
- When will I complete this goal?

You may have heard of the SMART acronym, but I've found that while many nod when I talk about it, few actually use it. The reason? It's hard.

Dreaming is fun, but when you start clarifying your goals you are forced to come face to face with the fact that they will require effort and sacrifice.

It's easy to say, "I'm going to save more money," but it's hard to make and follow a concrete plan that will lead to you saving money. As hard as it can be, clarifying your goals is a necessary first step to making them happen.

Asking those questions to define your goal can create a lot of motivation and excitement. Once you finish clarifying your goal, you can almost taste what it will feel like to complete it. You'll already be thinking of what you'll need to do next to get you

> *Dreaming is fun, but when you start clarifying your goals you are forced to come face to face with the fact that they will require effort and sacrifice.*

there. But hold your horses. Don't skip to the planning phase just yet. Now that you've written your goal clearly, it's time to evaluate it. Remember, the goal of goals is the glory of God. Whatever your goal is, you need to make sure it truly will act as a waypoint on your journey to bring God glory with your life. Evaluation saves you from chasing goals that aren't worth your time or God's resources.

Here are a few questions that I find helpful for evaluating my goals. First, does this goal line up with Scripture? You certainly don't want to pursue goals that are downright sinful or unworthy of a Christian. Second, does this goal line up with my giftings? Third, what are my motives in seeking this goal? Am I chasing that career change mostly for prideful reasons? Is my reason for seeking a pay raise so I can better provide for my family, or is it because I've made an idol out of money? Fourth, how will I bring God glory through this goal? Often, asking this question might make you abandon a goal. That's okay. In fact, you should consider that a good thing if it happens.

Management theorist Russell Ackoff used to say that many of our problems are the result of being efficient at the wrong things. In one interview, he said, "The curious thing is the righter you do the wrong thing the wronger you become. If you're doing the wrong thing and you make a mistake and correct it you become wronger. So it's better to do the right thing wrong than the wrong thing right. Almost every major social problem that confronts us today is a consequence of trying to do the wrong things righter."[3]

The only thing worse than being unproductive is being productive at the wrong things. How sad it would be to set your sights on a goal and pursue it with all your might, only to find it was something you shouldn't have been doing in the first place. That's why it's wise to pause and seriously evaluate your goals before you jump in and start working on them.

However, I find that evaluating a goal doesn't usually cause me to abandon it entirely. Often the goal just needs to be modified slightly. Take the example of weight loss. There are selfish, even sinful, reasons to want to get in shape. Maybe you want to attract the attention of the opposite sex, or perhaps you want to get ripped so you can finally beat up your high school bully. Those are bad motives, but the evaluation questions can help expose them. Then you can confess the sinful motives and reframe the same goal with a more God-honoring foundation. Instead, you might say, "I want to get in shape because my body is a temple of the Holy Spirit and because it is the most important tool in my productivity arsenal. To be healthy means to be more useful in serving God and others." Now that's a good motivation! Same goal, different reason.

The final step of evaluating your goal is to pray over it. How quickly we rush into plans without fully committing them to the Lord! Before you even take the first step toward your goal, commit your plans to the Lord (Prov. 16:3). If you feel ashamed to bring your goal before the Lord in prayer, that may be a sign that it isn't something you should be pursuing. Christians set on glorifying God won't dare to embark on a new objective without first seeking the Lord's wisdom and blessing.

2. Plan Your Habits

When I first started my blog, my writing was very sporadic. Sometimes I'd post five articles per week; other times I wouldn't upload one for months. I wanted to have a successful blog—I'd even set a SMART goal and defined what success at blogging would look like. But I was inconsistent in my progress. One day I was complaining about it to my friend. I told him, "I want my blog to grow, and I know that means publishing at least one article per week. But I just can't seem to get myself to do it regularly." My friend proposed a simple plan. He said,

"Why don't you write your first draft on Mondays, edit on Tuesdays, and post it on Wednesdays?" It worked! I had begun with a clearly defined goal, but I didn't have a plan for what I would do each day to reach it. To turn goals into progress, you need to plan your habits.

You'll have a lot of motivation right after writing and evaluating your goal, but don't use that motivation to start working on the goal yet. Many projects have failed because the initial inspiration was misspent by diving right in. Instead, capitalize on that momentum by making a plan that will sustain you even after the wave of willpower has passed. Goals must be transformed into plans and plans into habits.

GOAL   PLAN   HABITS

Figure 8.2: Goals to Plans to Habits

Your plan is the specific map of how you'll reach your goal. If your goal is to lose thirty pounds by July 1, then your plan might sound something like, "I will exercise on Mondays, Wednesdays, and Fridays in my basement at 7:00 p.m. and I will follow the X workout plan." Now you know what habits you are trying to ingrain. Habits are the specific, regular actions that will get you closer to your goal, and you'll need to train yourself to perform them regardless of how you feel. Here is where it can be tremendously helpful to utilize habits you already have.

Keystone habits are habits you already perform regularly that allow you to chain new habits onto them. In his book *The Power of Habit*, Charles Duhigg talks about how developing the keystone habit of exercise can have unintended ripple effects in other areas of your life.

When people start habitually exercising, even as infrequently as once a week, they start changing other, unrelated patterns in their lives, often unknowingly. Typically, people who exercise start eating better and becoming more productive at work. They smoke less and show more patience with colleagues and family. They use their credit cards less frequently and say they feel less stressed. It's not completely clear why. . . . "Exercise spills over," said James Prochaska, a University of Rhode Island researcher. "There's something about it that makes other good habits easier."[4]

Exercise is a great keystone habit, and so is the morning routine we talked about in practice one. When I'm trying to build a new habit, the first place I look to implement it is during my morning routine. If I can piggyback off a habit that's already working, my new habit is much more likely to stick.[5]

3. Enlist Accountability

There's a reason why people who have a gym partner exercise more frequently, why writers' groups exist, and why Alcoholics Anonymous uses sponsors. Accountability gets results. You are much more likely to reach your goals if you get someone to keep you accountable.

The best place to begin your search for an accountability partner is in your church family. Part of God's design for the church is that we would spur one another on (Heb. 10:24). If you can find another believer who has a similar goal he or she wants to reach, you can help each other stay encouraged and on target. But if you aren't able to find someone in your local church, the internet can also be a great source of accountability.

After having written on the topic of Christianity and productivity for several years, in 2021 I launched a community for like-minded believers called Redeeming Productivity Academy. One of the unexpected blessings of creating Redeeming Productivity Academy was the accountability it created. By bringing together a group of believers committed to personal productivity from all around the world, we inadvertently created an incredible support group for God-glorifying growth. Members have repeatedly told me that one of their favorite parts of being in the academy is the accountability they get from their fellow members, and that's been my experience as well. Even when I am thousands of miles away from someone, just knowing that I have someone who is committed to helping me reach my goals for the glory of God is an incredible encouragement. Besides, when you reach a goal alongside someone else, the victory tastes that much sweeter.

DOMAINS OF STEWARDSHIP

Finally, I want to address the question of *where to set goals.* Throughout this book, I've emphasized that productivity should be viewed in the category of stewardship, but sometimes it's hard to know exactly what parts of our lives we should be most focused on stewarding. After all, we have many different areas of responsibility. I call these our domains of stewardship. Distinct from goals, projects, and tasks, these domains are ongoing areas of responsibility which God has charged us to steward for His glory.

Most people's domains of stewardship look something like this:

- Spiritual
- Relationships
- Calling
- Health
- Finances
- Recreation

Yours may look a little different depending on your circumstances and stage of life, but most of us are responsible for our walk with the Lord, family and friends, career or calling, our personal health, money matters, and getting adequate rest and recreation. And if we are stewards of these domains, we should be seeing results in each of them for God's glory.

Being aware of each domain of stewardship helps you set goals in all areas of life. If you only set goals in a few areas, your other responsibilities are likely to be neglected and unfruitful. For example, only setting goals within the domain of your calling or career could result in fractures in your family, walk with the Lord, or physical health. Faithful stewardship is about taking responsibility for *all* that the Lord has entrusted to us.

It may be helpful to see how the different elements of productivity we've talked about fit together. Remember, our main objective is to be faithful in all that we do in such a way that God is made to look worthy

Figure 8.3: The Productivity Pyramid

of praise. This is what it means to glorify God. So if you picture a pyramid, God's glory is at the top. Under God's glory is domains. These are the areas we will steward to bring God glory. Under domains are goals, which we set to help us steward our domains well. Under goals are projects, used to make incremental progress toward our long-term goals. Finally, at the base of the pyramid are our tasks and habits. These make up the day-to-day actions we take that help us move the needle on the projects. Being a productive Christian means paying attention to each of these layers so that they build on one another, resulting in a life that is fully focused on bringing God glory.

CHOOSING YOUR OWN ADVENTURE

Before we move on to the next chapter, I want to address the question of the appropriateness of planning for Christians. You might be tracking with all this goal setting stuff but still thinking, "Isn't it presumptuous of me to set goals?" or "Isn't planning not leaving room for God to do what He wants in my life?" I have encountered many productivity-minded Christians who practice the very things we are talking about in this book yet still feel a little guilty about it. They have a vague sense that instead of planning, the more God-honoring thing to do would be to let life unfold however it will, as if refusing to make big choices in life is somehow more spiritual. Somewhere along the line, they've picked up the notion that planning is arrogant. But planning is not presumption, it's wisdom.

Most of our lives are spent being told what to do. When we are kids, our parents tell us when to go to bed and when to wake up, what to eat, where to go, and even when to bathe. When we get to school age, our teachers tell us this assignment is due next week, that class trip is on Thursday, and baseball practice is at 4 p.m. For many of us, this same hand-holding continues into adulthood at our jobs. "Here's your work, it needs to be done by this date." And it's rather infrequently that we face really big decisions where the choice is left entirely up to us.

When Kim and I had our first child, I remember how strange it felt when the staff let us walk out of the hospital with him. *Shouldn't someone have to sign off on this? We can just take him?* I've heard countless other new parents recount the same feeling of overwhelming responsibility, but what scared me the most about it was the autonomy. I wasn't just responsible for raising this kid. I was responsible for *deciding* how to raise him.

When we get handed the reins to make our own choices, we often don't know what to do, but we can encounter the same kind of discomfort when we presume to set goals for ourselves. It can feel almost wrong to simply make a plan and go for it. Many wonder, "Shouldn't I be getting approval from someone first?" I saw this hesitancy when I worked in college ministry. Almost every young adult I worked with had nearly crippling anxiety over "finding the will of God for my life."

This stress is certainly compounded by the analysis paralysis we spoke of earlier. In a world of endless options, it's hard enough to know which toothpaste to buy, much less what career path to choose. But it's worse for Christians, because many of us have somewhere absorbed the notion that it's unspiritual to choose. We would rather someone to tell us, "God wants you to be a doctor." Without a sign from heaven or some authority figure telling us what to do, we often push big life decisions onto others or delay until providence makes the choice for us. But I'm convinced that when it comes to stewarding our lives, we have far more autonomy than we might think. And that's by design.

Recently I was reading the parable of the talents in Matthew 25, and something struck me that I'd never noticed before. The master doesn't tell the stewards how to invest the talents. He just tells them to take care of his money (vv. 14–15). He doesn't give them detailed instructions or an investment strategy. Yet it was the stewards who proactively and creatively invested what was entrusted to them who were commended in the end (vv. 16–17; 21–23). And it was the uncreative, unadventurous, treasure-burying third steward who was rejected by the master for his faithlessness (vv. 24–30). I don't think this is a minor detail of the story. Faithful stewards choose their own adventure. They take what God has given them and they prayerfully seek to employ it to glorify God in the best way possible. Stewardship isn't about playing it safe; it's about taking full responsibility and then taking action. But there's a proper attitude that should accompany this kind of responsibility. We must be humble planners.

Presumptuous planning is indeed condemned in the Scriptures. James has this to say about arrogantly making our plans irrespective of God:

> Come now, you who say, "Today or tomorrow we will go into such and such a town and spend a year there and trade and make a profit"—yet you do not know what tomorrow will bring. What is your life? For you are a mist that appears for a little time and then vanishes. Instead you ought to say, "If the Lord wills, we will live and do this or that." As it is, you boast in your arrogance. All such boasting is evil. (James 4:13–16)

Notice that it is not planning that is condemned in that passage, but *boastful* planning. Planning done irrespective of the Lord is arrogance. When we set goals for our life without bathing them in prayer or aligning them with our chief end of glorifying God, we are indeed being presumptuous in our planning. God-honoring goal setting acknowledges that "the heart of man plans his way, but the LORD establishes his steps" (Prov. 16:9). That certainly doesn't mean don't plan;

it means don't plan arrogantly.

In fact, elsewhere the Scriptures hold up planning as an example of God-honoring wisdom. "Go to the ant, O sluggard; consider her ways, and be wise. Without having any chief, officer, or ruler, she prepares her bread in summer and gathers her food in harvest" (Prov. 6:6–8). No one is telling the ant what to do; nevertheless, she fulfills her responsibilities. She chooses her own adventure. Interestingly, her example is held up in contrast to the sluggard who refuses to get up, plan, and take action (vv. 9–11).

Part of the reason we don't plan is that we fear taking on that much responsibility. We're afraid our plans might fail. But setting goals as a Christians means acknowledging that our plans may indeed be thwarted, and that's okay. Because when your main goal is to glorify God through your goals, you don't begrudge providence, you embrace it. "Many are the plans in the mind of a man, but it is the purpose of the LORD that will stand" (Prov. 19:21). Christians who plan with that attitude honor God, and they also grow in their faith. Even if you set your goals with humility, there are times when God's plans for you are different. Often this results in a season of trial and disappointment, but we know trials, and even the destruction of our best laid plans works together for our good and spiritual growth (Rom. 8:29; 1 Peter 1:7).

Goals are good if they ultimately seek to glorify God. Sometimes Christians can discount the value of planning because it seems unspiritual, but planning and goal setting are just wisdom in action. God expects us to use our noggins to find the best ways to steward our lives for Him. The principles in this chapter won't guarantee the success of your temporal goals, but they will make success more likely. And if you really do seek to glorify God with your goals, even if the goal itself fails, you will have still succeeded.

PILLAR 5

THE MOTIVATION FOR PRODUCTIVITY

You Will Give an Account to God

——— – – ———

Thus far we have seen how the foundation for a Christian's view of productivity differs from the world regarding its origin, purpose, content, and power. A believer's desire to be productive comes from knowing that he or she belongs to God, and the purpose of all their productive efforts is to bring Him glory. Believers fulfill that purpose through bearing the fruit of good works, and they know that productivity empowered by God is that which truly counts. The fifth pillar of Christian productivity concerns our ongoing motivation for being productive. If we want to redeem productivity, we need to understand that someday we will give an account for our lives to God. The world says to be productive so you can get more from this life. The Bible says to be productive so you can gain more in the next life.

In this chapter, we'll look at some common bad motivations for being productive. These are the motives secular productivity enthusiasts most often appeal to, but Christians can be prone to believe them as well. Then, we'll examine how God has presented heavenly reward as the proper motive for a Christian's productivity. We'll also see how a desire for heavenly reward is not a mercenary motive but the very essence of the type of faith that pleases God. Finally, we'll look at how every aspect of our productivity can be motivated by and contribute to our eternal reward.

BAD MOTIVES FOR PRODUCTIVITY

I love motivational posters. You know the ones; they have a photograph of a mountain or an eagle above a single word like "Teamwork" or "Discipline." I find these posters humorous because they're usually found in spaces that are completely incongruous with the scenes they depict. Whenever I come across motivational posters in the hallways of a school or office building, I can't help but imagine what the people who put them up must have been thinking as they hung them there. I like to think their minds were filled with visions of people pausing before the poster and suddenly being swept away from their beige surroundings bathed in fluorescent light, enraptured by the perfect marriage of stock image and cliché before them. Then, inspired, they return to their desks, ready to take on the world!

While it's easy to poke fun at motivational posters or other cheesy attempts to inspire, the fact that artwork like this adorns the walls of schools and office buildings is proof that everyone knows how important motivation is for productivity. However, people need much more than a poster to motivate them to excellence.

Everyone is driven by something. We sometimes describe certain people as motivated and others as unmotivated, but strictly speaking, there's no such thing as an unmotivated person. The difference is just in *what* is motivating him or her. You might call your unshaven,

Netflix-bingeing, unemployed brother-in-law unambitious, and you might be right. But he's not unmotivated. More likely, the reason he's not working is because he's more motivated by a desire for comfort than for cash. You can make judgments about the quality of that motivation, but it is a motivation nonetheless.

While studying the topic of gaming addiction for a previous project, I was surprised to discover that video game addicts tend to be highly motivated people. The problem isn't that video game addiction represents a lack of motivation; it's just a misplaced motivation. When a person becomes overly motivated by in-game rewards, he or she begins to neglect real-life rewards. And therein lies the key to motivation: everyone is driven by the promise of reward. Whether it's a good feeling, financial benefit, or fame, we are motivated by the reward we crave.

We all face slumps in our productivity from time to time, so how do we motivate ourselves to keep going even when it's hard? If you search the productivity world for help on the issue of motivation, you'll find information on topics like self-discipline, habits, and various psychological theories that all promise to help you develop more productive drive. The problem, of course, is that secular productivity gurus would have us focus on the wrong kinds of rewards to keep us motivated.

The Reward of Riches

Most productivity books are geared toward businesspeople. Whether it's getting a promotion, building a million-dollar business, or retiring early, the promise of secular productivity is a life of financial prosperity. Money is assumed to be the obvious incentive for being productive. But this motivation presents a problem for Christians because Scriptures warn us that love of money is dangerous. "But those who desire to be rich fall into temptation, into a snare, into many senseless and harmful desires that plunge people into ruin and destruction. For the love of money is a root of all kinds of evils. It is through this craving that some have wandered away from the faith and pierced themselves with many pangs" (1 Tim. 6:9–10). We can't let the reward of riches be the motivation for our productivity.

The Promise of Peace

The second common motivation for productivity is the promise of peace. Maybe you're looking to productivity not primarily for wealth but for control. Life is chaotic, and you feel that if you could just get a bit more organized, you would finally find some peace. You may tell yourself that you aren't as bad as *those people* who want to get rich so they can live a lavish lifestyle. No, you just want enough to be financially free so you don't have to work. You want productivity to earn you time, not money.

Indeed, productivity often does lessen feelings of stress and worry. A well-ordered life tends to lead to less anxiety as we become better at keeping our commitments. But if believers hold up peace as our main motive for being productive, we may overlook the peace we already have through faith in Jesus Christ. Even peace can become an idolatrous motivation for productivity.

The Praise of People

A third bad motivation for productivity is the praise of men. Perhaps you aren't seeking riches or peace, you just want others to notice your accomplishments. This is a pernicious motivation because it can look so much like faithfulness. For example, consider the guy who always stays late to help clean up after events at church or the woman who shows up before her boss to work each day. Those are good things in and of themselves, but if the reason for those productive efforts is just to look good to others, that's a problem. When you do a good thing with a bad motive, you are doing a bad thing.

This motivation is sadly very common in ministry contexts. When you aren't working hard for a paycheck, it's easy to think that your motives must be pure. Deep down, however, the force driving you to be productive isn't a desire for God's commendation but for people to look at your tireless effort and say, "What a great person!" This is the motivation that drives empty religion; this was the motivation of the Pharisees! If you get organized, set goals, manage your tasks, and work hard just so people will think highly of you, you've missed the mark. The purpose of productivity is the glory of God, *not* your own glory. The praise of people is yet another bad motivation for productivity.

The Lure of Legacy

The fourth bad motivation for productivity is the lure of legacy. This motivation is just the praise of men in a more palatable form. Some people are motivated not by concern about money, peace, or what others around them will think but instead by a desire to leave a legacy. This sounds much nobler than being productive for the praise of men, but the lure of legacy is just a similar motivation in a time machine.

Of course, we all want to be thought well of after we're dead and gone, and legacy is not wholly a bad thing. But the lure of legacy must not be the chief motivation of a Christian. We cannot be motivated to productivity by the hope that others will make a positive assessment of our life when we're gone. Instead, we need to be motivated by how God will assess our life.

THE RIGHT MOTIVATION

Despite the many bad motivations that can drive productivity, we would be mistaken if we concluded that motivation itself was the problem, as if the antidote to bad motivations for productivity is to not want anything at all. Unfortunately, when it comes to motivation and ambition, I think that's the conclusion many Christians have drawn.

It's very easy to mock the self-help genre as a bunch of hokey get-rich schemes for wannabe entrepreneurs, but as we've seen throughout this book, ambition itself is not a sin. It's the *why* of our ambition that matters most. And motivation is the why behind ambition. J. Oswald Sanders put it this way: "Desiring to excel is not a sin. It is motivation that determines ambition's character. Our Lord never taught against the urge to high achievement, but He did expose and condemn unworthy motivation."[1] So what should motivate a productive Christian, then? Productive Christians are motivated by eternal reward.

You were made to seek reward, but it's not the reward of riches, peace, praise, or legacy that you were made for. These are all anemic half-forms of the true reward you were made to be motivated by. In fact, if you look closely at each of these bad motivations, you'll notice a perverted version of eternal reward. For example, our heavenly reward is referred to as eternal riches, which is different from the money we accumulate in this life. Similarly, we long for the ultimate peace of being at home with Christ, not merely the temporal peace of the absence of responsibilities. And when it comes to the approval of people or our legacy, what we were really made for is the "Well done" that comes from God, not man. All these motivations are bad not because they are too ambitious but because they are not ambitious enough.

Reward Is Right

Purpose and motivation are braided together. Our purpose is to glorify God, which is itself a powerful motivation for productivity. But it becomes even stronger when we recognize that our highest good is also tied up in this endeavor. God rewards us for living lives that glorify Him. At first this can sound kind of self-centered. Should we really be obeying just for the sake of reward? Doesn't Jesus say we should be good for goodness' sake? No, that's Santa Claus. Over and over again the Bible commends those saints who sought to obey God, not in spite of but *because of* the reward they were seeking.

Abraham is commended because He believed God, and that faith was credited to him as righteousness (Gen. 15:6, 22; Rom. 4:3). But what exactly was it that Abraham believed God about? It was the promise of reward (Gen. 12:1–3; Heb. 11:11). Likewise, in Hebrews 11:24–26, Moses is said to have rejected "the fleeting pleasures of sin," instead choosing "the reproach of Christ." What was Moses's motivation for making this seemingly foolish trade of pleasure for reproach? "He was looking to the reward" (v. 26). Being motivated by reward is not wrong when the reward is the promises of God. In fact, the promise of reward is presented to New Testament believers as a proper motivation for productivity in good works as well: "And let us not grow weary of doing good, for in due season we will reap, if we do not give up" (Gal. 6:9).

Indeed, God promises to reward us for our good works. We are to do our work not for the praise of men, but for the praise of God, "knowing that whatever good anyone does, this he will receive back from the Lord" (Eph. 6:8). Romans 2:6 says, "[God] will render to each one according to his works." And what is it He will render or repay us with? "Glory and honor and peace for everyone who does good" (v. 10). We are also rewarded for self-denial (Matt. 16:24–27), having compassion on those in need (Luke 14:13–14), loving our enemies (Luke 6:35), being generous (Matt. 19:21), enduring hardship and persecution in faith (Heb. 10:34–36; Luke 6:22–23), and living a godly life (2 Peter 3:11–14). I love how simply John Bunyan put it: "Whatever good thing you do for Him, if done according to the Word, is laid up for you as treasure in chests and coffers, to be brought out to be rewarded before both men and angels, to your eternal comfort."[2]

I'm not talking about working for your salvation. Our salvation is by grace alone through faith alone, not by our works (Eph. 2:8–9). Yet the Bible repeatedly says that faithful obedience will be rewarded in eternity (Pss. 19:11; 58:11; Prov. 11:18; Matt. 6:1–5; Col. 3:4). Everyone who believes on the name of Jesus Christ will go to be with Him in heaven, but we will each receive varying degrees of reward depending on how faithful we were with what we were given to steward.

These degrees of reward are what the apostle Paul is talking about in 1 Corinthians 3:10–15 when he speaks about building on the foundation of Jesus Christ:

> According to the grace of God given to me, like a skilled master builder I laid a foundation, and someone else is building upon it. Let each one take care how he builds upon it. For no one can lay a foundation other than that which is laid, which is Jesus Christ. Now if anyone builds on the foundation with gold, silver, precious stones, wood, hay, straw—each one's work will become manifest, for the Day will disclose it, because it will be revealed by fire, and the fire will test what sort of work each one has done. If the work that anyone has built on the foundation survives, he will receive a reward. If anyone's work is burned up, he will suffer loss, though he himself will be saved, but only as through fire.

Here Paul envisions the Christian life as a building. The gospel of Jesus Christ is the foundation. Since our faith is in Him and His finished work on the cross, we can be confident that our building will survive the fires of judgment. In the Father's eyes, Jesus' perfectly righteous works are credited to our account by faith. However, we build on this foundation with our own works, not in a way that contributes to our salvation but in ways that contribute to our eternal reward.

The day of judgment will reveal the quality of our works in this life, and we will be rewarded to the degree we stewarded our lives well. "For the Day will disclose it" (1 Cor. 3:13). When God looks on our lives, all who have trusted in the works of Christ will be saved, but the worthless stuff we've done will be burned up, no more valuable than wood, hay, and stubble are in a fire. But there are good works of a certain quality that will stand the testing flames, and we will be rewarded for these. These are the works we want to produce. This is the content of our productivity that we talked about in chapter 5. The promise of reward for these good works is the motivation behind all our productivity as Christians.

Too Heavenly Minded?

Sometimes people will paint a critical picture of this view of work, which is so focused on eternal reward. They'll throw around terms like the "Protestant work ethic" as pejoratives. They'll say we're too heavenly minded to be of any earthly good. They'll claim it's inherently selfish or isolationist and that it removes people's obligation to serve those around them. To all that I say, "Phooey!" It's nonsense. I agree with Randy Alcorn when he says, "This missing ingredient in the lives of many Christians today is motivation."[3] And the Scriptures hold out the promise of eternal reward as the highest motivation for good works. I don't think Christians lack motivation because they are too heavenly minded but because they are not heavenly minded enough.

Our obedience to God and our service to others should not be motivated by such paltry incentives like what we will gain in this life, whether temporal riches, passing peace, or the praise of others. Christians should live lives that overflow abundantly with the fruit of good works because we are unashamedly looking to the reward. Like Paul, we should race that we might obtain a crown that will last forever (1 Cor. 9:24–25). Christians should be the most productive people in the world because we are motivated by the greatest reward.

I get up every day and seek to make the most of every moment, not because I hope to become a millionaire or because I think that if I can just get organized enough, I'll have some peace. I'm not trying to optimize every hour because I care what people think of me, or even because I care what my kids or grandkids will think of my life. I wake up every morning and I get to work because by God's grace I want to live a life that is jam-packed with good works done in His power and for His glory. So, in my job, in my home, in my hobbies, and at my church, I want to manage my time, energy, and resources the best I possibly can. That's not just any motivation to be productive; that is the very best reason to be productive. It's the reason God gives us for being productive. Productive Christians get things done because we are motivated by eternal reward.

Being motivated by reward to be productive for God's glory is not a selfish, mercenary motivation. It's the very stuff of faith. Like Abraham, Moses, and all the saints who came before us, we walk in faith. When we are faithful because we believe God rewards faithfulness, we are believing the promises of God.

Branches, Stewards & Rewards

There are two passages we have continually returned to throughout this book, Jesus' metaphor of the true vine and His parable of the talents. Both texts also demonstrate that eternal reward ought to be the driving motivation for our productivity.

First, as we saw in John 15, when Jesus spoke of His disciples abiding in Him and thereby bearing much fruit, He was referring to the fruit of good works. But if you keep reading, you notice another peculiar quality about this fruit: it doesn't rot. In verse 16, Jesus continues, "You did not choose me, but I chose you and appointed you that you should go and bear fruit *and that your fruit should abide*" (emphasis mine). That our "fruit should abide" means that it should remain. It's not going anywhere. Works done for Jesus are works that last forever. When we seek to be productive for His purposes, in His power, and for His glory, we will discover that what we're really doing is storing up treasure in heaven.

Second, in the parable of the talents, you'll remember that the reward for faithful stewardship wasn't merely a pat on the back. The master commended the first two stewards saying, "Well done, good and faithful servant." But he continued with a promise, "You have been faithful over a little; I will set you over much. Enter into the joy of your master" (Matt. 25:21, 23). Faithful stewardship results in reward. When we are faithful to steward all that God has given us in this life, we will be rewarded in the next. I can think of no greater motivation to be a productive steward than the promise of commendation and reward from our Lord and Savior Jesus Christ!

YOUR PRODUCTIVITY MATTERS ETERNALLY

I wonder what would happen if we really believed that our daily productivity mattered on the eternal timeline. What if we really believed every moment of our day was a stewardship from God? What would happen if we viewed our jobs not merely as a necessary evil to make a paycheck but as a glorious opportunity to store up treasure in heaven?

Imagine how the simple mental shift of thinking about our work in terms of eternal reward might impact every aspect of what we do. Surely it would make us work with more integrity, because we'd know that even if our boss doesn't see our hard work, God does. It would give us more joy in even the most menial tasks, because we'd know that, ultimately, we aren't working for money or the praise of men but for an eternal reward. We would pay closer attention to the words of Paul when he said, "Therefore, my beloved brothers, be steadfast, immovable, always abounding in the work of the Lord, knowing that in the Lord your labor is not in vain" (1 Cor. 15:58). If your work is done in faith, your labor will never be in vain because faithfulness is rewarded in heaven, regardless of who sees your work or what you're paid for it.

A NEGATIVE & POSITIVE MOTIVATION

We need to admit that having our work stand before God can be a terrifying proposition, but we should recognize that the judgment we are talking about here concerns reward, not punishment. There is a judgment that every person on earth will face, and that day won't be pretty. Peter talks about how those who persist in wickedness and do not trust in Jesus Christ will meet Him: "But they will give account to him who is ready to judge the living and the dead" (1 Peter 4:5; see also Matt. 25:31–33). But the Scriptures speak of a second judgment for believers (2 Cor. 5:10; Rom. 14:10, 12). This is not a judgment unto punishment but unto reward.

Many Christians seem to have believed the notion that once you get saved, life is just a matter of waiting around for heaven. We avoid the "big" sins, of course, but because we are under grace and can't lose our salvation, we think the stakes aren't really that high. As a result, we float through life aimless and unproductive. Why wear yourself out if the bag is already secured? Yes, we are waiting for Jesus' return, but God has also promised great reward for His faithful servants (Rev.

11:18), and He is not stingy with how He rewards loyalty. He is generous, promising to return "a hundred times" (Matt. 19:29). As Randy Alcorn notes, "This is ten thousand percent interest, a return far out of proportion to the amount invested."[4]

There's a reward ceremony coming, and I want more than a participation trophy. That's what should get us out of the bed every day. That's what should fuel our productivity. We should be like Jonathan Edwards, who in his twenty-second resolution wrote, "Resolved, to endeavor to obtain for myself as much happiness, in the other world, as I possibly can, with all the power; might, vigor, and vehemence, yea violence, I am capable of, or can bring myself to exert, in any way that can be thought of."[5]

Nothing but eternal reward will give us the passion, the motivation, and the will to sacrifice temporal pleasures for the sake of faithful productivity. I don't care about productivity because it can help me earn a bigger income, or because it feels good to have my life organized. I care about productivity because I'm dead set on redeeming the time of these evil days (Eph. 5:16). I care because I know there is a day appointed on which my Lord will return to judge my works. And I mean by all His power that He mightily works in me to live a life that results in my hearing those blessed words uttered from His lips, "Well done good and faithful servant, you have been faithful in a little, I will set you over much."

A productivity that pleases God is one that is motivated by eternal reward. We were wired for reward, but the danger in undiscerningly reading productivity literature is that we might trade the God-designed motivation of eternal reward for the paltry incentive of temporal reward. If we really believe that our treasure is in heaven, then our work, productivity, and the motivation that fuels us should reflect that truth.

No one who strives to be productive for God's glory in pursuit of eternal reward will be disappointed. So let us press on. And when we come to the end of our lives, may we be able to say with John Calvin, "It is my happiness that I have served Him who never fails to reward His servants to the full extent of His promise."[6]

Next, we will look at practice number five, a practical strategy for keeping this truth salient in your mind so that it can constantly be fueling your productivity.

PRACTICE 5

WRITE YOUR
WELL DONE

———— – – ————

In the previous chapter, we saw that the best motivation for personal productivity is eternal reward. Now, I'll show you a method for keeping that motivation at the forefront of your mind. We'll discover why a well-defined vision for your life is so important, see how most approaches to this practice fall short, and learn exactly how to write an eternally minded vision statement that will help you stay focused on what matters most.

THE POWER OF VISION

When I was in college, one of the men who discipled me taught me the practice of creating a personal vision statement—a short, pointed statement reflecting the values that I wanted my life to be about. That was a long time ago, and my original vision statement has gone through many iterations and modifications over the years. But it's remarkable to me that the core of what I wrote down all those years ago has remained relatively unaltered. And when I reflect on the many twists and turns my life has taken, I can see in hindsight just how much that vision statement has helped me stay focused on glorifying God.

When I say vision, I'm not talking about a literal vision from God. I'm talking about having a vision for your life in the same way a company has a vision statement to codify its values. Developing such a statement is an exercise in clarifying exactly what you're about. As I've tried to emphasize throughout this book, Christians shouldn't simply float through life aimlessly. As God's children, we have a clear purpose for our lives, we've been uniquely gifted to fulfill it, and our faithfulness in that mission will result in our eternal reward. As long as you submit your ambitions and plans to the will of God, having clarity about your values and the particular way you're designed to glorify God is a very good thing. Your vision, then, is simply the theme to your life. God may change that theme, but writing a vision statement is simply the practice of articulating what you believe that theme is with as much clarity as you have right now.

Having a laser focus on our particular mission in life is also an admission of our own finitude. We can't do it all, and God doesn't expect us to, but we can do one thing really well. Companies recognize this—in addition to stating what the company *is* about, a corporate vision statement also states what it is *not* about. A narrow focus is necessary because one of the biggest enemies of productivity is mission drift. This is as true in the life of an individual Christian as it is in a company. We only have so much time to do what God has put us here to do. Speaking on the power of singular focus in the face of limited time, Charles Spurgeon once said,

> We must have only one aim. Had we plenty of time, we might
> try two or three schemes at once, though even then we should

most probably fail for want of concentrating our energies; but as we have very little time, we had better economize it by attending to one thing. The man who devotes all his thought and strength to the accomplishment of one reasonable object is generally successful.[1]

Many people in the Bible had clear visions for what they had been called to as well. Abraham sought a better land and a great nation (Gen. 12:1–2), and Joseph sought to preserve the people in the land through his work in Egypt (Gen. 37:5–8). Moses was about delivering God's people from Egypt (Ex. 3:1–3; 7–8). Jesus was about the salvation of mankind (Luke 19:10), and Paul set his sights on the conversion of the Gentiles (Rom. 15:20). Knowing who you are and what you're about will enable you to productively serve God.

WHY YOU SHOULD HAVE A VISION STATEMENT

There are at least three key benefits of a specific, written personal vision statement. First, it helps you make decisions. When two great opportunities present themselves, having a clear vision statement allows you to ask, "Which one of these is more aligned with who God made me to be and where I want to go?"

Second, a vision statement can help you determine your long-term and short-term goals. It enables you to always draw a line from glorifying God to what you're doing right now, today. You are connecting your purpose to your domain of stewardship, goals, projects, and what you're doing right at this moment. When these things are defined, you can have confidence that what you're doing right now is exactly what you should be doing.

Third, having a written vision statement reminds you of your motivation when things get tough. Not every day is satisfying or productive. When you feel frustrated or lost and start asking, "Why am I even doing this?" your vision statement has a ready answer. But not all vision statements are created equal.

THE LONGEST-TERM VISION

The concept of a personal vision statement has been around for a while. Many productivity programs will walk you through the construction of a long-term vision for your life. But most of these plans are built on the bad motivations we talked about in the previous chapter. I do believe the vision statement can be redeemed, however. We just need to address some of the inadequacies of secular vision statements.

Some plans for creating a vision statement focus on one-, five-, and ten-year visions. These shorter-term vision statements can certainly be helpful, but if we are talking about a vision for your whole life, we need to think a little more long-term. There's one type of vision statement that I've always found intriguing: writing your own eulogy. I first came across this concept in the book *Living Forward* by Daniel Harkavy and Michael Hyatt.[2] Writing your own eulogy makes you envision what you hope people will say about you after you're gone. After writing it, you are supposed to ask yourself, "When I examine the current trajectory of my life, can I reasonably assume people might say those things about me?" If not, then you know where to make changes and set goals to correct your course.

Focusing on your own death does help you overcome some of the typical temporal motivations that can creep into a vision statement. Instead of getting hung up on money, personal happiness, or present reputation, you are forced to ask bigger questions. How might my kids describe me at my funeral? My wife? My employer? My church? Would they say positive things? Would the positive things they say reflect the values I hold? If not, what can I change to ensure my life is headed toward a eulogy I can be proud of?

But there's something about writing your own eulogy that's always rubbed me the wrong way, and it's not the morbidity of it. Maybe you already caught it. Writing your eulogy is the perfect expression of a preoccupation with personal legacy, one of the bad motivations we talked about in the last chapter. The legacy I leave is not unimportant, but some day all the things I've done and built on earth will dissolve into eternity. How I spend my life and invest in my relationships must, therefore, be primarily for an audience of One. As we saw in the previous chapter, the productive Christian's chief motivation is a desire for eternal reward.

If we are going to have vision statements, therefore, they need to stretch beyond five years, ten years, and even our own death! We need a vision statement that will help us keep an eternal perspective on productivity, something less about what people will say about us and more about what Christ will say to us. We need a tool that will draw our eyes heavenward even when our heads and hands are buried in the most mundane work, a vision that will act as a compass when we aren't sure where to go next. We need to imagine our "Well done, good and faithful servant."

IMAGINING YOUR "WELL DONE"

I propose that you produce a written statement envisioning what you hope the Lord will say to you when you meet Him. Now, this might make you uncomfortable, just like writing a eulogy should make you a little uncomfortable; nevertheless, I've found it to be a very helpful tool for assessing the current trajectory of my life. I frequently return to my "well done" statement, and doing so instantly helps me reorient my priorities and assess my goals. Before I walk you through creating your own, I'll show you what my own "well done" statement says:

> Well done, good and faithful servant. You have been faithful to walk with Me daily, reading My Word and seeking Me in prayer. You have been faithful with your family, loving Kim as I loved My church, and raising your children up in wisdom and My instruction. You have been faithful to your calling of helping My brothers and sisters become more faithful stewards for My Father's glory. You have been faithful with your health, stewarding your body as the temple of the Holy Spirit, eating healthy and exercising regularly. You have been faithful with your finances, not being foolish and not hoarding My money as if it were your own, but using it to care for your family, give to My church, and provide for the needs of others. And you've been faithful in your recreation, respecting your need for rest as a finite creature and making time to enjoy My creation, eating, and drinking to My glory. Because you have been faithful in these little things, I will set you over much. Enter the joy of your Master.

This is simply an exercise in imagination. You aren't pretending that you've been given this vision by divine revelation, and you aren't trying to put words in God's mouth. Notice how my statement is laden with biblical language. That's because I want this statement to represent what I believe, based on Scripture, God values most from my stewardship in these areas. Writing out my "well done" helps me personalize the expectations the Bible says God has of me. Anyone who has given much thought to meeting Christ has wondered and hoped for what He would say to them. This exercise is just putting words to those hopes, and the resulting clarity can then act as a touchstone for testing your goals and the opportunities that come your way.

Creating Your Statement

There is a simple formula for writing your own "well done" statement. Start with the words the master in the parable of the talents spoke to the faithful stewards: "Well done, good and faithful servant. You have been faithful . . ." Then, insert how you envision faithfulness might look in each of the domains of stewardship we discussed in chapter 8:

- Spiritual
- Relationships
- Calling
- Health
- Finances
- Recreation

If you look back at my "well done" statement, you'll see that I've simply included a sentence or two for each domain of stewardship, written from the perspective of Jesus. For example, "You have been faithful to your family, loving Kim as I loved My church, and raising your children up in wisdom and My instruction" covers my relationships. You could add another sentence to include friends, coworkers, or extended family, but since you'll be looking at this statement every day, it's wise to keep it succinct.

Once you've written out your statement, review it a few times to make sure it captures what you really see as most important to God in each of those domains. But don't obsess over it, because you'll revisit and refine your "well done" over time. Mine has gone through many edits over the years as my priorities have changed and new seasons of life emerge.

Ask Yourself Some Questions

Once you have written your "well done" statement the way you want it, look at what you wrote and honestly ask yourself these three questions:

Is my life currently on a path to hearing, "Well done, good and faithful servant"? This one is a high-level gut check. You might survey your statement and realize that you aren't being faithful in nearly any of those areas—you aren't being responsible to your calling; you aren't caring for your relationships; you aren't even walking with the Lord daily. Asking this question can be incredibly humbling. Good. That's what it's for. You've just held up a mirror to your life. If you don't like what you see, praise God for grace! Repent of where you're falling short and ask for the Lord's help to become the faithful man or woman He wants you to be.

What areas might Christ say I've been a good steward in? Chances are you'll feel that you're doing well in at least one or two areas. That's good! This exercise isn't about finding things to beat yourself up about. Give thanks to God for enabling you to be faithful and fruitful in those areas. In addition, consider exactly why you're being faithful in those areas and how you can continue to be, as well as what goals you could set to pursue even greater faithfulness in those areas.

What areas would Christ say I have not been as faithful in as I should? Maybe you're knocking it out of the park in terms of stewarding your physical body, but your finances are a mess. You aren't treating your money like it's the Lord's. Again, repent specifically for these things and ask for God's help to be more faithful with them. Then, go back to practice four and develop a goal or goals that will help you become more faithful in this area. Employ your task management system to create and execute projects to reach that goal. Organize your environment to make that goal easier to reach, and utilize your morning routine to stay consistent. If you've been following this book closely, you now have an arsenal of productivity tools to put to use to enable you to be more faithful in areas where you've identified shortcomings. And that's the whole point of this question—it's an assessment. If you assess yourself and find you need to make changes but don't actually take action, this whole endeavor is pointless.

REVIEWING & REFINING YOUR STATEMENT

As with writing your goals, writing down your "well done" is only half the battle. You need to review it regularly. I recommend two types of reviews, daily and long-term. Long-term reviews should be done at least annually, though quarterly is even better (I recommend scheduling long-term reviews as appointments on your calendar). During these long-term reviews, you simply examine your "well done" statement closely and update it as needed. If you want help with this, I lead a free annual planning webinar every December for everyone on the Redeeming Productivity mailing list. Part of that training is reviewing the previous year through this lens, adjusting your vision, and setting goals for the coming year to ensure you are being faithful in every domain.

The second type of review is a daily review. I read my "well done" every morning as part of my POWER Mornings routine. I don't assess or update it during these times; I'm simply using it to ground myself in the big picture of why I'm here. You could write your "well done" statement in the front of your journal, keep a printed copy on your desk, or include it in a template if you use a digital journaling tool. What matters is making it part of your daily habits. Reviewing your "well done" every day will protect you from becoming too myopic. It's far too easy to fall back into laziness, chase productivity for productivity's sake, or become busy because that's what others expect of us. Revisiting your eternal hope every single morning is the spiritual reset forgetful creatures like us need.

In the busyness and chaos of life, creating a personal "well done" statement is just one more practical strategy for keeping what's most important ever before your eyes. By never going a day without reminding ourselves of the purpose and reward of faithful stewardship, we will keep ourselves from forgetting why we're doing what we're doing.

EPILOGUE

Recently, I had Dr. Kelly Kapic, author of the book *You're Only Human*, on my podcast. Dr. Kapic has written and talked a lot about the subject of finitude—the fact that we humans are not infinite like God is. We are limited in what we can do, and that is by design. As we were concluding the interview, I asked him if he had anything he would like to share with productivity-minded believers, and this is what he said: "God is calling us to be human, not superhuman." His point was that it's far too easy to transform an interest in productivity into a quest for perfection. When you take seriously God's call to be fruitful and redeem the time for Him, it's easy to beat yourself up when you inevitably fall short. So, I want to leave you with this final piece of encouragement:

You are going to fail.

Yes, you are going to fail. You are going to overcommit, you're going to break promises, you're going to fail to meet your goals, you're going to waste time, you're going to procrastinate, you're going to have unfinished to-do lists, and you will end many days feeling entirely unproductive. And that's okay, for two reasons.

First, even if sin had never entered this world, you still would not be able to get it all done. You're a creature, not the Creator. Finitude was baked into the goodness of creation, and God doesn't begrudge you for not having an infinite capacity to get things done. He just calls you to be faithful with whatever He's left to your charge. Christian productivity isn't a quest to do everything we can possibly do. It's a quest to be faithful with what God has given us. And that means accepting and respecting that you have limits, you need rest, and you will fail often.

Second, you are going to be sinfully unfaithful at times with your time, energy, and opportunities. And that's okay too. It's okay because by faith in Jesus Christ we have forgiveness for our sins—past, present, and future. When you fall short, confess it to God, thank Him for His grace, and then get right back up and try to be faithful again tomorrow. You aren't going to get it perfect, but it's okay because we serve a God who is Himself perfect.

That's what redeeming productivity is all about—seeking to be faithful in good works for the glory of our great God. The Christian life is a long journey with much stumbling along the way, but the prize for faithfully and fruitfully stewarding your life will be worth the best of your productive efforts. Don't give up.

"And let us not grow weary of doing good, for in due season we will reap, if we do not give up." (Gal. 6:9)

ACKNOWLEDGMENTS

Even though I've been thinking and writing on this subject for nearly six years, crafting my ideas into a book was far more difficult than I thought it would be. And it would not have been possible without my incredible wife, Kim. From talking out concepts with me, editing early drafts, advising on cover options, cooking insanely delicious meals, and watching our kiddos so I could write, her support and encouragement helped make this book happen. Thank you so much, dear.

Thanks to Moody Publishers for taking a chance on me. You held my hand every step of the way and made the arduous process of writing a book clear and even a little bit fun. Special thanks to Drew Dyck for his encouragement, clear communication, and for giving me this opportunity. Thanks to Charles Snyder for your editing. You did me the invaluable service of making me sound less like an idiot. Not an easy feat.

Thanks to Jessica Mohr, whose editing and feedback on the early chapters and book proposal were invaluable. She helped me trick Moody Publishers into thinking I could actually write a book. Her advice and keen theological mind also helped me clarify my thinking on many critical sections and shaped the direction of the book as a whole.

I also want to thank Tim Challies, who graciously wrote the foreword to this book. His kind support over the years and his own book on productivity, *Do More Better*, encouraged me to continually dive deeper into how God's Word shapes what we think about work and productivity.

Thank you to all the listeners and readers of my podcast and blog. Your feedback, questions, and encouraging emails over the years helped me refine the ideas in this book. And I especially want to thank the members of Redeeming Productivity Academy and my supporters on Patreon. Your support, both moral and financial, has enabled me to explore these ideas as my full-time job. Inasmuch as my ministry has been a blessing to you, you have been a double blessing to me. Thank you.

Finally, thank you to Joey Cusenza, Adam Ford, Andrew McNeill, Bryan Murphy, James Parker, Matt Russell, Peter Sammons, and Miska Wilhelmsson. Each of you have significantly influenced my understanding of what it means to steward our time well for the glory of God.

NOTES

Chapter 1: The Origin of Productivity: You Belong to God

1. Darren Hardy, *The Compound Effect: Jumpstart Your Income, Your Life, Your Success* (New York: Vanguard Press, 2010), 108.

2. *Merriam-Webster*, s.v. "hedonism (*n.*)," last updated May 27, 2022, https://www.merriam-webster.com/dictionary/hedonism.

3. Charles Spurgeon, "Redemption and Its Claims," *The Metropolitan Tabernacle Pulpit, Vol. 20*, March 8, 1874, https://www.spurgeon.org/resource-library/sermons/redemption-and-its-claims/#flipbook/.

4. R. C. Sproul, *John: An Expositional Commentary* (Sanford, FL: Reformation Trust, 2009), 286.

Chapter 2: Craft Your Morning Routine

1. Charles Duhigg, *The Power of Habit: Why We Do What We Do in Life and Business* (New York: Random House, 2014), 100.

2. "Christians throughout history have deemed it appropriate to give the firstfruits of the week to God in order to acknowledge his ownership of the whole, just as they do with income." Mark Dever, *The Church: The Gospel Made Visible* (Nashville: B&H Publishing Group, 2012), 1732, Kindle.

3. "Adm. McRaven Urges Graduates to Find Courage to Change the World," *UT News,* May 16, 2014, https://news.utexas.edu/2014/05/16/mcraven-urges-graduates-to-find-courage-to-change-the-world/.

4. Andrew A. Bonar, *The Biography of Robert Murray M'Cheyne* (Edinburgh: Banner of Truth Trust, 2012), 20.

5. Drake Baer, "9 Books Billionaire Warren Buffett Thinks Everyone Should Read," *Business Insider*, September 2, 2014, https://www.businessinsider.com/warren-buffett-favorite-business-books-2014-8.

Chapter 3: The Purpose of Productivity: You Exist to Glorify God

1. David Allen, *Getting Things Done: The Art of Stress-Free Productivity* (New York: Penguin Books, 2015), 225.

2. Stephen R. Covey, *The 7 Habits of Highly Effective People: Powerful Lessons in Personal Change* (New York: Simon & Schuster, 1989).

3. Stephen R. Covey, A. Roger Merrill, and Rebecca R. Merrill, *First Things First: To Live, to Love, to Learn, to Leave a Legacy* (New York: Free Press, 1994).

4. "I have found in speaking to various non-LDS groups in different cultures that we can teach and testify of many gospel principles if we are careful in selecting words which carry our meaning but come from their experience and frame of mind." Stephen R. Covey, *The Divine Center* (Harrisonburg, VA: R. R. Donnelley and Sons, 1982), 240.

5. "The Westminster Shorter Catechism," The Presbytery of the United States, accessed April 20, 2022, https://www.westminsterconfession.org/resources/confessional-standards/the-westminster-shorter-catechism/.

6. John MacArthur and Richard Mayhue, *Biblical Doctrine: A Systematic Summary of Bible Truth* (Wheaton, IL: Crossway, 2017), 226–28.

7. In the Old Testament, the phrase "The glory of Yahweh appeared" frequently appears alongside verbs signifying a visible sight (Ex. 16:7, 10; 24:16, 17; 40:34, 35; Lev. 9:6, 23; Num. 14:10; 16:19, 42; 20:6; Deut. 5:24). For example, when the glory of Yahweh was on Mount Sinai, the text says, "The appearance of the glory of the LORD was like a devouring fire on top of the mountain in the sight of the people of Israel" (Ex. 24:17).

8. Thomas Watson, *A Body of Divinity* (Edinburgh: Banner of Truth Trust, 1958), 6.

9. Ibid., 7.

10. Abraham Kuyper, *Lectures on Calvinism* (Grand Rapids, MI: Eerdmans, 1931), 53.

11. Thomas Watson, *A Body of Divinity*, 6.

Chapter 4: Get Organized

1. Sönke Ahrens, *How to Take Smart Notes: One Simple Technique to Boost Writing, Learning and Thinking* (n.p.: Createspace Independent Publishing, 2017), 16–17, Kindle.

2. James Clear, *Atomic Habits: Tiny Changes, Remarkable Results* (New York: Avery, 2018), 82.

3. Anne-Laure Le Cunff, "Environmental Psychology: What to Put on Your Bedside Table," *Ness Labs*, September 16, 2019, https://nesslabs.com/bedside-table.

4. Tim Challies, *Do More Better: A Practical Guide to Productivity* (Minneapolis: Cruciform Press, 2015), 49.

Chapter 5: The Content of Productivity: You Were Saved to Bear Fruit for God

1. Jon M. Huntsman, *Winners Never Cheat: Everyday Values We Learned As Children but May Have Forgotten* (Upper Saddle River, NJ: Pearson Education, 2005), 44.

2. See Os Guinness's *Carpe Diem Redeemed* (Downers Grove, IL: IVP Books, 2019) for an excellent exploration about how our view of time shapes the way we live.

3. John MacArthur and Richard Mayhue, *Biblical Doctrine: A Systematic Summary of Bible Truth* (Wheaton, IL: Crossway, 2017), 378–79. See Matt. 7:16–20; 12:33; Luke 6:43–44; Gal. 5:19–23.

4. Matt Perman, *What's Best Next: How the Gospel Transforms the Way You Get Things Done* (Grand Rapids, MI: Zondervan, 2014), 77.

5. Ibid., 74.

Chapter 6: Track Your Commitments

1. J. Mathes, M. Schredl, and A. S. Göritz, "Frequency of Typical Dream Themes in Most Recent Dreams: An Online Study," *Dreaming* 24, no. 1 (2014): 57–66, https://doi.org/10.1037/a0035857.

2. "What is GTD?," Getting Things Done, accessed February 28, 2022, https://gettingthingsdone.com/what-is-gtd/.

3. Sönke Ahrens, *How to Take Smart Notes: One Simple Technique to Boost Writing, Learning and Thinking* (n.p.: Createspace Independent Publishing, 2017), 69, Kindle.

4. Ibid., 70.

5. I must acknowledge the deep influence David Allen's Getting Things Done system has had on what I present here. If you are familiar with Allen's GTD methodology, much of this won't be new to you. But I have made some significant modifications to account for a biblical anthropology and what I've found to be most effective in practice.

6. For a list of my recommended task management systems, check out https://www.redeemingproductivity.com/task-managers.

7. Special thanks to Donnie Halbgewachs for helping come up with this acronym. My original acronym spelled TEASES (trusted, external, actionable, simple, engaging, singular). But that was too embarrassing to put in print.

8. David Allen, *Getting Things Done: The Art of Stress-Free Productivity* (New York: Penguin Books, 2015), 21.

Chapter 7: The Source of Productivity: You Are Uniquely Gifted by God

1. John MacArthur and Richard Mayhue, *Biblical Doctrine: A Systematic Summary of Bible Truth* (Wheaton, IL: Crossway, 2017), 379.

Chapter 8: Set Your Goals

1. Gary Keller and Jay Papasan, *The ONE Thing: The Surprisingly Simple Truth Behind Extraordinary Results* (La Vergne, TN: Bard Press, 2013), 154.

2. George T. Doran, "There's a S.M.A.R.T. Way to Write Management's Goals and Objectives," *Management Review* (November 1981).

3. Phyllis Haynes, "Russell Ackoff / Haynes Media Works," YouTube video, 9:48, January 11, 2010, https://www.youtube.com/watch?v=MzS5V5-0VsA.

4. Charles Duhigg, *The Power of Habit: Why We Do What We Do in Life and Business* (New York: Random House, 2012), 109.

5. For more on how the Bible talks about habit development check out Dr. Greg Gifford's *Heart & Habits: How We Change for Good* (Woodlands, TX: Kress Biblical Resources, 2021).

Chapter 9: The Motivation for Productivity: You Will Give an Account to God

1. J. Oswald Sanders, *Spiritual Leadership: Principles of Excellence for Every Believer* (Chicago: Moody Publishers, 2017), 13.

2. Randy Alcorn, *Money, Possessions, and Eternity* (Carol Stream, IL: Tyndale House Publishers, 2003), 123.

3. Ibid., 129.

4. Ibid., 123.

5. Jonathan Edwards, "The Resolutions of Jonathan Edwards," *Desiring God*, December 30, 2006, https://www.desiringgod. org/articles/the-resolutions-of-jonathan-edwards.

6. Alcorn, *Money, Possessions, and Eternity*, 123.

Chapter 10: Write Your Well Done

1. Charles Spurgeon, "The Time is Short," *Metropolitan Tabernacle Pulpit Volume 49*, December 10, 1903, https://www.spurgeon. org/resource-library/sermons/the-time-is-short/#flipbook/.

2. Michael Hyatt and Daniel Harkavy, *Living Forward: A Proven Plan to Stop Drifting and Get the Life You Want* (Grand Rapids, MI: Baker Books, 2016). Donald Miller also recommends writing your own eulogy in *Hero on a Mission: A Path to a Meaningful Life* (New York: HarperCollins Leadership, 2022).

BE MORE PRODUCTIVE, SET BETTER GOALS, AND LIVE LIFE ON PURPOSE

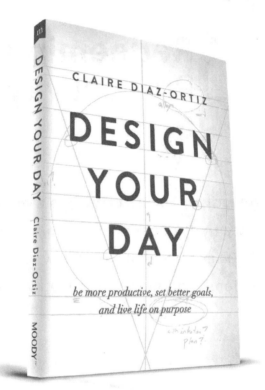